BUILDING POWER FROM BELOW

Building Power from Below

Chilean Workers Take On Walmart

Carolina Bank Muñoz

ILR Press
an imprint of
Cornell University Press
Ithaca and London

First published 2017 by Cornell University Press

Printed in the United States of America

Library of Congress Cataloging-in-Publication Data

Names: Bank Muñoz, Carolina, 1975– author.
Title: Building power from below : Chilean workers take on Walmart / Carolina Bank Muñoz.
Description: Ithaca : ILR Press, an imprint of Cornell University Press, 2017. | Includes bibliographical references and index.
Identifiers: LCCN 2017011395 (print) | LCCN 2017013993 (ebook) | ISBN 9781501714689 (epub/mobi) | ISBN 9781501714771 (pdf) | ISBN 9781501712883 | ISBN 9781501712883 (cloth : alk. paper) | ISBN 9781501712890 (pbk. : alk. paper)
Subjects: LCSH: Wal-Mart (Firm)—Employees—Labor unions— Organizing—Chile. | Discount houses (Retail trade)—Employees— Labor unions—Organizing—Chile. | Labor unions—Organizing— Chile. | Labor movement—Chile.
Classification: LCC HF5429.215.C5 (ebook) | LCC HF5429.215.C5 .B36 2017 (print) | DDC 331.88/113811490983—dc23
LC record available at https://lccn.loc.gov/2017011395

Cornell University Press strives to use environmentally responsible suppliers and materials to the fullest extent possible in the publishing of its books. Such materials include vegetable-based, low-VOC inks and acid-free papers that are recycled, totally chlorine-free, or partly composed of nonwood fibers. For further information, visit our website at cornellpress.cornell.edu.

For the Chilean Walmart workers who have dedicated their lives to organizing from below.

For Emilio who on a daily basis gives me hope for the future.

CONTENTS

ACKNOWLEDGMENTS

All research projects benefit from the participation and encouragement of many different people and institutions, this project is no different. This book would never have come to fruition without the participation of dozens of Walmart Chile workers, union leaders, and suppliers. I am indebted to all those workers who took many hours out of their busy schedules to allow me to interview them, observe their workplace environment, and participate in union meetings. I am especially thankful to Sandra Neida, Natalia Duque, Cristian González Santibáñez, Juan Vergara, Esteban Zúñiga, Rodrigo Villagra, and Jorge Pizarro who not only opened doors, but a whole new world. I would also like to thank organizers and researchers at the UFCW who put me in initial contact with people in the Chilean labor movement. Although I am often critical of the union, it comes from a deep commitment to building a better labor movement in the United States.

Over the course of five years, I have participated in two different writing groups. Tamara Mose and Greg Smithsimon—my colleagues at

Brooklyn College—pushed me to turn my fieldwork into a book, when I thought I only had a good story. Tamara played an especially important role holding me accountable to the project, always asking me how much work I had done on the book. The second writing group with Penny Lewis, Rachel Sherman, and Stephanie Luce encouraged me to sharpen my analytical lens and think about the implications of my work. Penny, Rachel, and Stephanie offered invaluable guidance, a sharp eye, and much encouragement. I am forever grateful for their astute sociological thinking.

I have also benefitted from the presentation of this work at the Race Workshop at the University of Chicago's Center for the Study of Race, Politics and Culture. Here I received excellent and engaging critique from Tianna Paschel, Virgina Parks, and Alfredo Gonzalez, among others in the workshop. I also participated in the Politics and Protest Workshop at the CUNY Graduate Center in 2015–2016, allowing me to think through and fine tune ideas. I am particularly grateful to John Krinsky and Jim Jasper for their insightful comments.

The Fulbright Scholars program funded my stay in Chile in 2011, thus allowing me to conduct research and teach at the Alberto Hurtado University. It so happened that the semester I was scheduled to teach was the same semester that Chilean university students went on strike for over nine months, calling for free higher education. I was incredibly fortunate to be in Chile at the right time and witness the reemergence of an important social movement. I am also grateful to Brooklyn College for approving my sabbatical request at the same time as I was awarded the Fulbright. During the course of this research I received the Claire and Leonard Tow Research Travel Fellowship, as well as three PSC-CUNY grants. These different sources of funding allowed me to conduct follow-up research in Chile, as well as prepare the manuscript for publication.

I would be remiss to not mention Fran Benson's continuous support of my book ideas and research projects. I benefitted greatly from the comments of the two reviewers who read the manuscript for Cornell University Press. A special shout out goes to Joel Stillerman who wrote the most generous, critical, and on point review I have ever received. Karen Fein spent many hours editing the initial draft. I am appreciative for her sharp eye and attention to detail.

I am fortunate to have incredibly supportive colleagues in the sociology department and in the college as a whole. Many friends have also listened to me struggle with the ideas in this book, especially Juan DeLara, Tara Marray, Lisa Gallegos, Scott Melzer, Rigoberto Rodriguez, Belinda Lum, Edna Bonacich, Prudence Cumberbatch, Corey Robin, Namita Manohar, Ana Cardenas, Antonio Stetcher, and Bridget Kenny. My dad has played an invaluable role in supporting and expressing interest in my research. Most recently he asked me: "Am I going to get to read this book before I die?" I took this as a clue to wrap it up. I am also really fortunate to have amazing aunts, uncles, and cousins in Chile who welcomed me into their lives for seven months and made me feel like I had never left Chile. Special thanks to Ana Muñoz, Jaime Astudillo (Sr.), Anita Astudillo, Jorge Echeverría, Jaime Astudillo, Carola Aljaro, Gabriela Astudillo, Rosa Muñoz, Olga Muñoz, Hugo Muñoz (Sr.), Luz Quirland, Claudio Muñoz, Viviana Muñoz, Jorge Muñoz (Sr.), Caty Zanocco, Catalina Muñoz, Mauricio Muñoz, and Jorge Muñoz.

Finally, my partner Ted Levine has given me extensive comments on a number of chapters. Most important, he has parented Emilio every Sunday for the past year and a half so that I could complete the manuscript. Emilio, our son, demonstrated extraordinary patience and love as I completed this book.

Acronyms

AFL-CIO	American Federation of Labor-Congress of Industrial Organizations
AIFLD	American Institute for Free Labor Development
AWOC	Agricultural Workers Organizing Committee
CIA	Central Intelligence Agency
CNI	Central Nacional de Informaciones
CODELCO	Corporación Nacional del Cobre (National Copper Corporation)
CTC	Confederación de Trabajadores de Cobre (Copper Workers Confederation)
CTW	Change to Win Federation
CUT	Central Unitaria de Trabajadores (National Trade Union of Workers)
D&S	Distribución y Servicios (Distribution and Services)
ENCLA	Encuesta Laboral (Labor Census)

FENATRALID	Federación Nacional de Trabajadores Líder (National Federation of Líder Workers)
GFA	Global Framework Agreement
GUF	Global Union Federation
ILO	International Labor Organization
ITF	International Transport Workers Federation
LTS	Logística, Transportación y Servicios (Logistics, Transportation, and Services)
Madeco	Manufacturas de Cobre S.A. (Copper Manufacturers)
NLRA	National Labor Relations Act
NLRB	National Labor Relations Board
OECD	Organization for Economic Cooperation and Development
OSAL	Observatorio Social de América Latina (Social Observatory of Latin America)
OUR Walmart	Organization United for Respect at Walmart
SEIU	Service Employees International Union
SIL	Sindicato Interempresa Líder (Interenterprise Líder Union)
UFCW	United Food and Commercial Workers Union
UFW	United Farmworkers
UNI	Union Network International
UP	Unidad Popular (Popular Unity Party)

BUILDING POWER FROM BELOW

1

BEATING THE BULLY

On a cold and cloudy autumn morning in Santiago, Chile I set out for the lower middle class neighborhood of Matucana to attend my first Walmart protest. I took the subway and walked past auto body repair shops, small factories, and hardware stores. The Walmart Supercenter is located on the corner of two high traffic streets, several blocks away from the nearest residential neighborhood. It is by far the largest supermarket in the area, measuring over 75,000 square feet, an imposing building in a neighborhood of small shops.

That day—April 28, 2011—eighty Walmart workers, mostly young and middle-aged women came together to hold a union meeting in front of the Walmart Matucana store. This was the third *reunion en la calle* (street meeting) that workers across Santiago had organized. Workers were meeting in the street because Walmart had recently changed a long-standing policy that allowed them to hold lunchtime union meetings in the store. Walmart argued that if it allowed the union to have meetings in the store that it would then have to allow all kinds of groups to hold similar meetings.

Wait, a union at Walmart? Yes. The majority of Walmart's 38,000 workers in Chile are unionized. In fact, many workers across Walmart's global operations are unionized. In the case of Chile, Walmart had to agree to accept the unions as a condition of entry into the country when it bought majority share of the Chilean retail giant D&S in 2009. Even so, many more Chilean Walmart workers have been able to organize under Walmart proper over the last six years. Not having the right to have union meetings in the store during lunch might not strike a U.S. audience as significant, especially given Walmart's antiunionism in the United States, but in Chile this struck a nerve with workers and even members of the community. Having the ability to meet and discuss union business is considered a fundamental right in Chile.

In response to this new policy, Walmart workers and their unions decided to take matters into their own hands. Workers organized street meetings outside different Walmart stores all across Santiago. They made big banners that said "Así Nos Trata Walmart. Tenemos que Hacer Reuniones en la Calle" (This is how Walmart treats us. We have to have meetings in the street) and "Walmart Anti-Sindical" (Walmart is antiunion) and stood in the chilly weather for two hours right outside the entrance. They plugged in sound equipment inside the store and spoke on microphones about miserable working conditions at Walmart stores. As workers spoke up, both customers and other workers stopped and listened. Additional workers joined the meeting as they rotated shifts.

While the meeting was going on, Walmart managers (all middle-aged men) took note of the workers participating and wrote down names. They videotaped the entire meeting and forced security guards to stand next to workers to intimidate them. But these workers and union leaders were not intimidated. They showed their faces without any sign of hesitation or fear. At one point during the meeting, Walmart managers asked security to unplug the sound system. Eventually Walmart gave up, because workers just kept plugging it back in.

These street meetings and demonstrations are bold actions in the face of an antiunion employer. In order to participate in these kinds of mobilizing efforts, workers must first feel a sense of confidence and collective identity. In the case of Walmart Chile, a significant part of their confidence comes from participating in a democratic-militant union where they have a voice in shaping strategy and decision making. Their local level organizing and

Figure 1.1. Reunion en la Calle (street meeting). Photo by author.

small wins at their particular Walmart store have engaged them more in the daily life of the union and have made it easier to stand up to their boss. The local union president at Walmart Matucana, Sandra Neida, is a charismatic and energetic person committed to social movement unionism and democratic principles. At the meeting I attended, workers voted in favor of a 10 percent increase in dues in order to improve their capacity to fight against Walmart. They also pledged to find a location for a union office so that they could hold meetings without relying on their bosses for space inside the store, while at the same time maintaining the right to have meetings in the store whenever they deem it necessary. This meeting is one of many examples of how Chilean Walmart workers have taken control over their work lives and are successfully organizing against the transnational retail giant.

Worker Activism in the Face of Neoliberalism

There are two striking reasons that Walmart in Chile makes an interesting case study. First, it is notable that there is a union at all at Walmart Chile, and there are in fact many unions. By contrast, no union has been able to penetrate Walmart in the United States in over fifty years. Second, workers have organized the most powerful transnational corporation in the world in a country that has been described as the "cradle of neoliberalism" since the mid-1970s. And Chile, like the United States, has been suffering from a declining labor movement. So this advance within Walmart cannot simply be chalked up to a better national climate, or a more successful, or strong, labor movement.

The Rise of Walmart in the United States

Walmart, founded by Sam Walton in Bentonville, Arkansas in 1962, has over 4,000 stores in the United States alone, and another 6,283 across its global operations (Walmart 2014). What explains Walmart's rapid growth? Lichtenstein (2006) argues that the combination of the agricultural revolution in the American South, and a shift in the U.S. economy toward a neoliberal model guaranteed Walmart's unprecedented growth.

As geographer David Harvey argues, neoliberalism is fundamentally about the restoration of class power (Harvey 2005). His argument is based on the idea that global elites lost economic and financial power between the 1930s and the late 1960s. During this time period unions were strong and had effectively fought employers. The Great Depression propelled workers and their organizations to fight for the establishment of social security, unemployment benefits, welfare, and labor protections through the National Labor Relations Act (NLRA). By the early 1970s, the welfare state had taken its toll on profits, and elites needed to act to maintain and increase their class power. In short, then, neoliberalism is about a system of redistribution back to the one percent. In both the United States and Chile, neoliberalism is best characterized as an economic and social project driven by the support of free markets, free trade, deregulation, privatization, and austerity measures (Harvey 2005). In chapter 2 I discuss how the neoliberal project was implemented in Chile after the U.S.-sponsored military coup against Salvador Allende in 1973. In the United States itself, the shift to neoliberal economic policy is most associated with Ronald Reagan. His transformation of the business environment through privatization and deregulation changed the labor movement for decades to come. Of particular importance was Reagan's dismantling of strong antimonopoly legislation (Lynn 2006).

Prior to Reagan, legislation prevented the kind of growth Walmart has been able to achieve. At its peak, A&P, the closest competitor to Walmart, was only two times larger than its largest competitor. Many big firms of the twentieth century were repeatedly taken to court on monopoly charges, guaranteeing their limited control. However, Walmart has been allowed to expand exponentially with little constraint (Lynn 2006). This expansion has had a deleterious impact on its suppliers, who wield very little power over this giant, and workers who earn rock bottom wages.

In addition to neoliberal policies that have allowed Walmart's growth to reach epic proportions, the company has received unprecedented subsidies. According to the nonprofit organization Good Jobs First, "Walmart has received over $1.2 billion in tax breaks, free land, infrastructure assistance, low-cost financing, and outright grants from state and local governments across the country" (Mattera and Purinton 2004). These subsidies do not include the additional millions of dollars taxpayers are paying to provide health care and income support to Walmart workers due to Walmart's low wages. Because Walmart's wages are so low, many of its workers cannot afford Walmart-sponsored health insurance. In fact, Walmart wages are so low that many of its workers qualify for Medicaid and other social welfare programs, such as food stamps. Walmart workers have reported simultaneously filling out their employment applications along with public assistance applications. A 2004 study found Walmart workers' reliance on public assistance programs cost California taxpayers $86 million a year. Furthermore, "the families of Walmart employees in California utilize an estimated 40 percent more in tax-payer funded health care than the average for families of all large retail employees" (Dube and Jacobs 2004, 1). Walmart's growth and "everyday low prices" are a direct consequence of billions of dollars in direct and indirect subsidies.

Walmart has enjoyed exponential growth, while receiving unprecedented tax subsidies, without being required by the state to create good, stable, union jobs. On the contrary, Walmart has the reputation for being the most antiunion company in the world. U.S. unions have spent millions of dollars over the past two decades trying to unionize Walmart, yet each campaign has failed to yield a union at Walmart. The nonexistence of a union at Walmart cannot be attributed to lack of worker interest. Many workers would very much like to be represented by a union, as we have seen with various attempts at organizing a union, including OUR Walmart (Organization United for Respect at Walmart; Kroll 2013), but Walmart spends millions of dollars a year to ensure that U.S. stores will never be unionized. With their open-door policy and profit-sharing schemes, antiunion store manuals, expensive antiunion consultants, and captive audience meetings, Walmart utilizes an entire industry intended to keep stores union free (Lichtenstein 2007).

In addition to classic antiunion strategies, such as captive audience meetings, where workers are forced to listen to speeches and watch videos on the dangers of unions, and trainings for store managers on how to keep unions out of their stores, in 2012 Walmart took an unprecedented step in the surveillance of workers who are considered activists with OUR Walmart (Brown 2011; Eidelson 2012; Human Rights Watch 2007). OUR Walmart was founded in 2011, and initial funding came from the United Food & Commercial Workers International Union (UFCW), which aimed to unionize Walmart. Workers who joined OUR Walmart organizations primarily pushed for higher wages and better schedules. The organization used creative tactics by calling for a Black Friday strike at Walmart in 2012. Since then it has been responsible for leading Black Friday strikes every year. Although OUR Walmart has not had success in unionizing Walmart, their creative tactics and pressure were, in large part, responsible for forcing Walmart to increase their wages to $10 per hour in 2014.

The organization has also forced Walmart to grant a few other concessions. For example, in 2014 OUR Walmart members launched a campaign called "respect the bump" demanding Walmart to accommodate pregnant women with medical conditions, rather than forcing them into a leave of absence (OUR Walmart 2014). In 2015, journalists discovered that leading up to the first Black Friday strike, Walmart contracted Lockheed Martin, the world's largest defense contractor, to help with surveillance of OUR Walmart activists and to monitor who participated in the Black Friday strikes (Berfield 2015).

Walmart has been able to grow because of deregulation, tax benefits, trade policy, health policy, its locations in right to work states,[1] weak labor law, the general decline of the U.S. labor movement, and a collection of old and new union busting tactics. Today Walmart has all but saturated the rural, suburban, and exurban retail markets in the United States. However, it has been experiencing a growth crisis since 2004, especially since it has not been able to penetrate important urban markets such as New York City. In order for it to continue to grow it needs to move to urban markets and new markets globally. Its survival as a profitable company that trades well on the New York Stock Exchange hinges on an urban and global strategy. With those considerations in mind, Walmart went global.

Walmart Goes Global

Walmart began its international operations in 1991 with the opening of a Sam's Club near Mexico City (Walmart 2015). Within a few years, Walmart had opened hundreds of Walmart and Sam's Club stores throughout Mexico. As of 2015 it had retail operations in twenty-eight countries and employed over a million retail workers internationally (Walmart 2015). There are many more workers across Walmart's supply chain, but we do not have accurate information about these workers, because Walmart does not directly employ them. Walmart's international operations comprised about 30 percent of its net sales in 2015 (Walmart 2015). In Latin America, Walmart operates in Mexico (2,296 stores), Costa Rica

---

1. Right to work laws prohibit agreements between unions and employers. As of 2016, twenty-six states have right to work statutes in the United States.

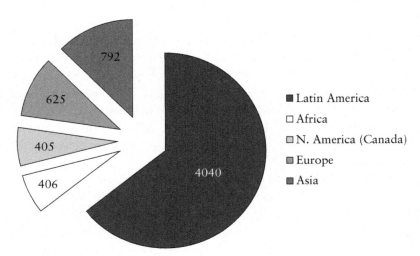

Figure 1.2. Walmart's international retail stores by region
Source: Author's calculation from www.walmartstores.com.

(219 stores), El Salvador (89 stores), Guatemala (217 stores), Hondu-
ras (81 stores), Nicaragua (86 stores), Brazil (559 stores), Argentina (107
stores), and as of 2016 its most recent acquisition in the region, Chile (386
stores). Clearly, Latin America presents a significant share of Walmart's
global operations.

As a global company Walmart has had varying success in different countries. It has failed in Germany and Japan but has had huge success in Latin
America. Since it first expanded overseas, Walmart has had to fine-tune its
approach. It has had to learn the hard lesson that it cannot simply replicate
the same model in every country. Institutional context and culture play
a significant role in the success and failure of Walmart as a global player
(Tilly 2006). What has become evident is that the Walmart model must be
flexible and respond to country specific circumstances. As such, in most
countries in the world, many of which have stronger labor laws than the
United States, Walmart has had to accept unions. Nonetheless, accepting
unions doesn't mean that Walmart has not tried to push the boundaries of
labor law and exert antiunion practices. It has taken particular kinds of
unions to be successful in fighting the worst of Walmart's policies.

Neoliberal reforms in Chile in the 1980s and 1990s restructured an entire society and created a new consumer culture that significantly facilitated the expansion first of D&S (Walmart's big box predecessor) and then of Walmart (see chapter 2). Given these dramatic changes in Chilean policy and culture, such significant worker mobilization against Walmart in Chile is striking. How do we explain workers' success in Chile, the cradle of neoliberalism, in challenging the world's largest and most anti-union corporation? What does an in-depth case study show us about how union democracy, autonomy, militancy, and strategic capacity are developed? And what are the implications for the United States and other countries organizing against Walmart? The answers to these questions lie in a deeper understanding of worker power.

Understanding Worker Power

At first glance Chile is an unlikely location for a strong worker movement. The dictatorship's legacy, coupled with a declining labor movement, does not make a good foundation. Paradoxically, it is precisely these conditions that have given rise to the unique opportunities that have facilitated worker activism in Walmart Chile.

Chilean workers are successfully organizing and bargaining at Walmart because they have learned to leverage power in resourceful ways. Walmart in Chile offers an interesting case study because it contains two different industries: retail, and warehouse. Retail and warehouse workers leverage their power in different ways, leading to different kinds of social power.

Types of Social Power

Since Chilean Walmart workers are already unionized, in this book I primarily focus on organized workers and their movements. As such, one of the main contributions of this book is to look at how different types of social power can be mobilized by different actors within one vertically integrated transnational corporation. The power that workers can leverage therefore affects strategy and outcomes. In previous work (Bank 2008), I've looked at the process of production and how different types of labor control (hegemonic and despotic) are used to produce and reproduce race and gender at the point of production. This project, by contrast, looks at how workers turn that labor control on its head by leveraging their social power to force Walmart to meet many of their demands.

What is social power? What does it mean to have social power? Like Jenkins (2002) and Frances Fox Piven and Richard Cloward (1978), I argue that social power means having the capacity for disruption. Effective strike threats can sometimes be just as powerful as actually going on strike. Jenkins (2002) argues that "oppressed people can only transcend the limitations imposed by elite decision-makers when they have the power to force the institutions they are confronting to accept their demands" (62). Furthermore, Piven and Cloward (1978) state that this disruptive power should not necessarily have to be rooted in institutions (such as unions) in order to be effective. In fact, they provocatively argue that it is when these movements organize into formal institutions/organizations that they begin to lose their power. They argue that it was disruptive action that made such movements as the Civil Rights, unemployed workers, and welfare rights movements—all without structural power—the most successful.

Yet another kind of power is power rooted in the cultural and public spheres, what Jennifer Chun (2009) calls "symbolic leverage." Chun argues that, "symbolic leverage aims to undermine official sources of authority, such as the law, and demand alternative applications of social justice" (2009, xiii). A prominent example of this kind of leverage is the Justice for Janitors Campaign that the International Service Workers Union waged in the late 1980s and 1990s, where the strength of the strike, came from elevating the poor working conditions of janitors to a moral level. Chun (2009) makes a particularly important intervention in the labor literature, which has historically privileged workers with structural power. In the United States this has largely taken the form of scholarship on the white, male working class. Yet the 1990s saw a revitalization of the U.S. labor movement by immigrants and women (Fantasia and Voss 2004; Milkman 2000; Milkman and Voss 2004,). Furthermore, the immigrants and women organizing were predominantly in the service sector. As a result, Chun (2009) articulates the need to think of power differently, especially among insecure, low-wage, and service sector workers. For these workers, symbolic leverage allows them to shift the balance of power and apply upward pressure in their demands for better working conditions.

Building on Jenkins (2002), Piven and Cloward (1978), and Chun (2009), I argue that there are two main types of social power: having the capacity for symbolic disruption and having the capacity for disrupting production. These are not necessarily mutually exclusive, though sometimes they are. Another way to think about it is power that disrupts the supply side (services) and power that disrupts the demand side (production). As Jenkins (2002, 62) argues, "social power must be based in some capacity of the group itself to *coerce* the decision-maker to make the changes they seek." Actions that we traditionally think of in relationship to labor movements, such as strikes, threats of strikes, direct action, and other strategies that stop production, slow down production or otherwise impact the employer's bottom line represent the capacity to disrupt production. Symbolic disruption also has the power to coerce employers to acquiesce to workers' demands, but uses different methods, such as shaming, public drama, and moral authority (Chun 2009). Even though the capacity for disrupting production and the capacity for symbolic disruption are not mutually exclusive, not all workers have the same access to these different kinds of disruption.

Determinants of Social Power

How do workers get social power? How do they attain the capacity for disruption? Erik Olin Wright (2000, 962) argues that power is "the capacity of individuals and organizations to realize class interests." He defines two kinds of worker power. The first, "associational" power, is the power that "results from the formation of collective organizations of workers" including political parties and unions. The second, "structural" power, "results simply from the location of workers in an economic system" (Wright 2000, 962). I agree with Wright (2000) about the importance of associational and structural power, but I deviate from his analysis that these are forms of power on their own. Rather, I argue that associational and structural power are determinants of social power. In other words, having a union, worker center, or political party on its own does not produce social power. It is what people do with those organizations that can create power. Similarly, structural location alone does not create power; it is how workers leverage their structural location that offers the opportunity to gain power. Under this conception, associational power allows for the production of both symbolic disruption and disruption of production, while structural power most commonly facilitates disruption of production. Since leveraging power implies some level of organization (associational power), I would additionally argue that workers must have associational power in order to leverage structural power. For example, Silver (2003), Bonacich and Wilson (2008) and others have pointed out that logistics workers occupy a key structural position in the supply chain and can bring global supply chains to a halt. However, if these workers are not organized, they are not going to leverage their structural power effectively.[2] Therefore, strong associational power, whether in unions or other working-class organizations, is instrumental to building the capacity for effective disruption and garnering increased social power.

Characteristics of Strong Associational Power

How do workers and their organizations build strong associational power? There are three central components: strategic capacity, union democracy, and militancy. Additionally, autonomy from political parties and state control, while not a condition for building strategic capacity, union democracy, and militancy, gives organizations the freedom to think independently.

Strategic Capacity   In his 2010 book, *Why David Sometimes Wins,* Marshall Ganz argues that the United Farm Workers of America (UFW) was able to more successfully organize farm workers and win against growers than the Teamsters Union or the Agricultural Workers Organizing Committee (AWOC) of the American Federation of Labor-Congress of Industrial Organizations (AFL-CIO) because they had the ability to "devise good strategy" or have strategic capacity. For Ganz,

---

2. The case studies in this book focus on workers who are already in unions, but I am not arguing that workers who are not in unions cannot leverage their structural location. When I talk about "organization" I mean that workers have a relatively strong sense of class-consciousness and the potential for collective action whether or not they belong to an organization.

An organization is more likely to achieve positive outcomes if it develops more effective strategy, and it is more likely to develop more effective strategy if its leaders can access diverse sources of salient information, employ heuristic processes, and demonstrate deep motivation—their strategic capacity. Variation in strategic capacity, again, derives from differences in leaders' life experience, networks and repertoires, and organizations' deliberative processes, resource flows, and accountability structures. (2000, 1019)

Much like Ganz, I argue that leadership and organization drive the Chilean Walmart warehouse and independent retail unions' ability to "devise good strategy" or have strategic capacity. Like the UFW in Ganz's discussion, the Chilean unionists I worked with, in both the retail and warehouse unions, were deeply motivated in their desire to build a powerful democratic grassroots union, particularly in Walmart, which was widely seen as an imperialist transnational corporation. They also benefitted from salient information and employed heuristic processes. For example, leveraging information about the sale of D&S to Walmart, and experimenting with different tactics. Differences in these organizations strategies (see chapter 3) stem from their structural location in addition to leadership and organization. In his model, Ganz (2000, 2010) points to the centrality of deliberative processes, resource flows, and accountability structures but only vaguely references the concept of union democracy. Here I differ from Ganz, because Walmart workers in Chile had union democracy as a central concern in the creation of their unions. For the Chilean unionists, in large part union democracy drives their organizations' deep motivation, deliberative processes, and accountability structures. But what exactly is meant by union democracy?

Union Democracy   The concept of union democracy has been hotly debated in the literature on union revitalization. There are many camps within the literature, with little consistency in how the concept is defined or considered. One set of scholars largely focuses on formal democratic processes such as representation, constitution, politics, and elections (Cook 1963; Dimick 2010; Edelstein and Warner 1976; Lipset et al. 1956; Stepan-Norris 1997; Stepan-Norris and Zeitlin 1989 and 1996). Within this group, scholars have vastly different takes on the role of formal democracy inside unions. The argument dates back at least sixty years, when

Lipset and colleagues (1956) derided the potential for unions to be democratic and representative organizations. Instead, they found that unions tended toward oligarchy. More than three decades later, Stepan-Norris (1997) and Stepan-Norris and Zeitlin (1989, 1996) presented a far more nuanced analysis, arguing that there are a multitude of paths for unions, and which path they take, whether tending toward democracy or oligarchy, is largely determined by internal political processes and factions.

By contrast, a more recent set of scholars focuses primarily on participatory democracy or active worker participation in campaigns and organizing (Bronfenbrenner and Friedman 1998; Hickey et al. 2010; Markowitz 1998, 1999; Milkman 2006; Sharpe 2004; Voss 2010; Voss and Gaston 2014; Voss and Sherman 2000). In this body of literature the central question of concern has been how do unions activate the rank and file? Most studies look at specific union campaigns, highlighting whether they use top-down or bottom-up strategies, or both. Their concern has been less on formal democracy and more on successful strategies for activating membership and winning.

Markowitz (1998) identifies the "blitz model" and the "comprehensive campaign model" as responses to employer antiunion hostility in the 1980s.[3] The UFCW developed the comprehensive campaign, which she describes as a campaign driven by the union, which relies on research to find unfavorable things about the employer and then uses the research as leverage to force the employer into a card check neutrality agreement, rather than a National Labor Relations Board election (which in the 1980s and 1990s was particularly unfavorable to workers). The comprehensive campaign required substantial secrecy and little worker participation.

By contrast, the blitz model developed by the Amalgamated Clothing and Textile Workers Union (now UNITE) focused heavily on worker participation, by getting workers to organize intensively for a short period of

---

3. The Blitz model is an organizing model where union staff are sent to a particular location that has a heated union battle to work on it for a short, intense period of time and then moves to the next location. The critique of the model is that workers do not develop a strong connection to the union because the staff member leaves once the campaign is won or lost. The comprehensive campaign is a different organizing model. Here the union organizing campaign is developed through the heavy integration of research, coalition building, political pressure, and legal pressure.

time and limiting the campaign period so as to catch employers off guard and unprepared. The blitz model also required some level of secrecy, especially in the beginning, but later it required much more rank-and-file involvement. Markowitz goes on to argue that both models excluded workers from actively participating in the collective bargaining agreement, but workers who participated in the blitz model pushed their union to let them participate in the process, whereas workers who were part of the comprehensive campaign simply assumed it was not their role to participate in bargaining. In the end the workers who participated in the blitz model, though somewhat discouraged after the campaign, ended up actively participating in the union a lot longer than workers who participated in the comprehensive campaign. In her study, Markowitz makes some interesting observations about the tensions between worker participation and union strategy.

Sharpe also sheds some light on the difficult balance between creating a space for worker participation and leadership and the union staff's need to "carefully manage and control the course of the campaign" (2004, 64). For Sharpe, the balance between building worker leadership and staff management is delicate, especially in the context of fighting antiunion employers with huge resources. Sharpe's piece captures the internal struggles that union staff face in having a strong desire to foster a democratic process among militant and engaged members, all the while trying to ensure winning the campaign.

In the blitz model, unions were extraordinarily effective at cultivating leadership and activism among the rank and file. Ultimately, strategic decisions were not made by rank-and-file workers, but rather by experts. The Sharpe (2004) and Markowitz (1998, 1999) studies especially point out the contradictions and tensions between union staff and the rank and file. On the one hand, most unions and union organizers want to cultivate a union culture that builds worker power and puts members in control of decision making. On the other hand, U.S. employers often wage incredibly hostile antiunion campaigns, and even once workers are organized, negotiating a collective bargaining agreement is extraordinarily difficult. As a result, U.S. labor campaigns, whether to form a union or negotiate a contract, become high-stakes endeavors. Because of the employer offensive against unions, many unions, particularly large unions with many resources, employ a small army of union professionals, including lawyers, organizers, researchers, lobbyists, and even finance specialists. As the daily work of the union becomes professionalized it often takes strategy and decision-making out of the hands of actual union members. Therefore there is a constant balancing act between building members' own power and ensuring success through a multi-pronged approach.

The final group of scholars writing about union democracy brings together formal democracy and member participation. These scholars argue that union democracy requires formal democratic processes, a high level of worker participation and engagement on a day-to-day basis, and significant power in the union's strategic decision-making and political process (Lévesque et al. 2005; Levi et al. 2009; Moody 1997, 2007; Parker and Gruelle 1999; Walchuk 2011; Weinbaum 2004). In her three case studies of factory closures in Appalachia (Greenbrier, Acme, and General Electric), Eve Weinbaum makes a case for "successful failures." While all three grassroots movements in response to factory closures failed to bring back jobs, they were successful in that they deeply empowered workers. As a result of the campaigns workers gained hands-on skills in the areas of strategy, democratic processes, the global economy, and employer tactics. In many cases workers' direct control over their movements facilitated long-term participation in the labor movement. Weinbaum's study shows us how grassroots movements can be transformative, even if they are not successful. Similarly, Moody argues that democracy and militancy are the only ways to turn the U.S. labor movement around. Using Canadian data, Lévesque et al. (2005) find that union democracy is a key tool in addressing membership dissatisfaction and bringing together collective identities.

My discussion of union democracy relies on the approach of this third camp. What sets the independent Walmart unions apart from the other Chilean Walmart unions, Chile's mainstream labor movement, and many unions in the United States is their commitment to base-building, bottom-up strategy, democratic structures, and membership participation. What is particularly unique is that these unions are fighting the world's largest transnational corporation with nearly no resources. Unlike most unions in the United States, neither the warehouse or retail unions I worked with had paid staff or political, organizing, or education departments. The best resourced unions I worked with only had the luxury of a part-time attorney and release time for the president of the union, allowing her or him to attend to the daily aspects of running a union. Most of these unions do not even have offices. These unions are run by and for the rank and file. Union democracy has both influenced the strategic capacity of these organizations and also has helped build stronger associational power, since these organizations have the tools to coerce employers into meeting many of their demands.

Militancy   A third component that contributes to building strong associational power is militancy. By militancy, I mean confrontational, disruptive, direct action tactics that workers and their organizations use to coerce employers to meet their demands (Isaac and Christiansen 2002). These actions involve significant economic, legal, or political risk for actors and can include actions such as strikes, blockades, and sabotage. Measuring militancy is difficult, since not all actions are recorded and categorized. Scholars often use strikes as a variable to measure militancy. Of course there are severe limitations to the data, because often countries count only legal strikes in the official data. Despite its limitations, looking at strike data is helpful in gaining an understanding of waves of militancy.

Militant action has long been an important tool for unions to force their employers' hand. Historically, U.S. strikes have been effective at crippling employers. In the 1930s, autoworkers, port workers, and steel workers all waged important strikes (Lichtenstein 1995; Selvin 1996; Turrini 1997). U.S. labor law always included a provision that allowed employers to replace workers, but it was not until 1938 with the Supreme Court decision in *NLRB v. Mackay Radio & Telegraph Co.* that employers were essentially given the right to permanently replace striking workers. This Supreme Court decision had a significant impact on the strength of the strike. Nonetheless, U.S. strike activity was strong through the late 1940s, in fact labor unrest peaked in 1945–46, with over 5,000 strikes each year (Dubofsky 1995). However, U.S. strike action has dramatically declined since the mid-1970s. In 2009, the United States experienced an all-time low with only five strikes, and in 2015 there were twelve strikes, leaving about 47,000 workers idle (Bureau of Labor Statistics 2016).

At the same time as we see low levels of militant action in the United States, we see increasing labor militancy in the Global South. As Silver

(2003, 5) astutely points out, "while labor has been weakened in the locations from which productive capital emigrated, new working classes have been created and strengthened in the favored new sites of investment." Since 2010, for example, we have seen extraordinary mobilizations in Asia, particularly China.

Labor militancy contributes to a sense of collective identity, increased class-consciousness, and a sense of empowerment even when workers' actions and movements fail to produce benefits (Weinbaum 2004). As such, militancy helps to forge stronger relationships, high levels of motivation, lessons, and capacity, all of which contribute to stronger associational power.

Worker Power in Chile

As in the United States, workers in Chile have been consistently losing power since the mid-1970s (see chapter 2). It is especially counterintuitive that in a small country known for its probusiness climate that retail and warehouse workers have challenged Walmart, the world's most antiunion corporation. Yet Walmart workers in Chile have been leveraging power in creative ways and achieving gains at the same time that there has arguably been a decline in worker power overall. In this context, how did workers build power in the first place? How did they learn to leverage the power that they built?

Suffice it to say that workers' movements do not occur in a vacuum. In the mid-2000s, Chile witnessed an explosion of social movements, starting with protests led by high school students. In 2007 many commentators considered a wave of worker strikes to be the reemergence of the Chilean labor movement (Aravena and Núñez 2009). The Logística, Transporte, Servicios (LTS) union, representing warehouse workers, organized in 2006, and the independent retail workers' unions organized between 2006 and 2011. These unions shared a number of important characteristics. First, they all had a commitment to autonomy. None of the unions I worked with were interested in participating in the national labor federation (Central Unitaria de Trabajadores), nor were the leaders of the unions interested in furthering their careers through the socialist or communist political parties. They had a strong belief that the labor movement was weak, at least in part, because workers had been used as tools of the political elite and had received little in exchange for their political loyalties.[4]

Second, they all shared a commitment to building grassroots unions with a focus on union democracy and militancy. Many had negative experiences with corrupt or ineffectual unions. Some of them had union experiences prior to Walmart, while others had been members of Walmart's own corrupt union (see chapter 2) before breaking away and creating their own organizations. All of them were committed to building a different kind of labor organization, what they referred to as a *sindicato de verdad* (a real union) and a *sindicato de base* (a grassroots union). What they articulated clearly was that in order to build worker power, worker organizations had to be democratically driven from their bases. For these workers, building a democratic union meant giving decision-making power to the membership and allowing members to drive their union's agenda from below. In addition to union democracy, the union leaders I interviewed emphasized that in order to build power, workers needed to take risks and engage in militant action. They especially believed this was true in challenging Walmart, because they were well aware of Walmart's reputation as an antiunion employer.

The unions I worked with have all been successful in building worker power at Walmart and at negotiating good contracts. As autonomous unions they have been able to create the conditions for building strategic capacity, union democracy, and militancy. These characteristics have all contributed to building strong associational power. Yet important variances contribute to how and why these unions have succeeded. Ultimately, retail and warehouse workers have different kinds of social power and therefore leverage their resources differently.

Warehouse workers have a tremendous amount of structural power because of their unique position in the industry. Because there are only three central Walmart warehouses in Chile, if these workers go on strike

---

4. Unions in Chile have historically been considered beholden to political parties (particularly the communist and socialist parties). It is one of the ways in which they were able to create a significant role for themselves in shaping the Chilean democracy. However, they were unable to extract significant change at the level of government policy outside of those political parties (Angell 1972).

they can paralyze Walmart's distribution of goods. Since these workers have a union, they also have associational power. Still, the strength of associational power is directly correlated with the strength of the union. Walmart warehouse workers are represented by two unions. LTS, the union I worked with, represents 2,000 workers at the two main warehouses. The third warehouse, initially created to undermine LTS, was organized in 2014 by the parcel company DHL's union, for reasons having to do with subcontracting and tax identification numbers (see chapter 2 for a discussion of labor law). Walmart warehouse workers' combination of structural and associational power has led them to engage in classic disruption. They staged a powerful strike in 2006 that shaped the union's organization, strategic capacity, and union democracy. As a result of the power that they have built, they have made substantial economic advancements through collective bargaining. These include significant wage increases, vacation time, a union office, health and safety provisions, and more (see chapter 4).

Walmart retail workers are distributed across over 300 different stores, ranging from small corner stores with ten employees, to Walmart Supercenters with over 400 employees. Because of the labor code, these workers are also distributed across eighty different unions. In general, these workers have associational power, in that most Walmart retail workers are members of a union, but there are stronger and weaker unions within Walmart itself. Retail workers, however, as a whole have limited structural power. Nonetheless, even in retail, some structural power can be leveraged and is leveraged in terms of different occupations within the retail stores. Cashiers, butchers, bakers, and fishmongers have significantly more structural power than stockers, in part because they are seen as skilled labor and therefore harder to replace. The two retail federations I worked with represent about 4,000 members (across thirty different enterprise unions). FENATRALID, the oldest, was organized in 2006, while Federación Autónoma was created in 2010. In addition, there are three other federations, including a corrupt union that represents about 14,000 workers. FENATRALID, the Federación Autónoma, and the unions that belong to them have had success in breaking the corrupt union's weak pattern agreement, thereby raising wages and improving bonuses and benefits, though not nearly to the level of the warehouse workers' (see chapters 2 and 5). However, it is arguable that some of their most significant victories have

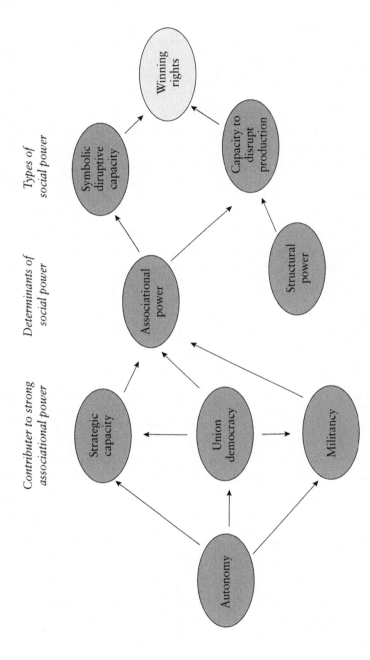

Contributer to strong
associational power

Determinants of
social power

Types of
social power

Figure 1.3. Worker power

been on noneconomic issues. In this way, the retail unions have used the strength of their associational power to wage campaigns that have used both symbolic disruption and classic disruption.

This case study illustrates how types and determinants of social power play out differently and interact in various ways in separate sites (retail and logistics) of a vertically integrated transnational corporation. The types of power available to workers influence their tactics and objectives. Making effective use of the types of power at hand, as have these autonomous unions, influences outcomes. They have been able to build democratic and militant unions with significant strategic capacity. These three factors—union democracy, militancy, and strategic capacity—have contributed to their strong associational power, which they have effectively leveraged through their symbolic disruptive capacity and their capacity for disrupting production. In addition, the warehouse workers benefit from structural power, which has allowed them to build capacity for disrupting production.

Methodology

In 2009, during a three-week visit to my family in Santiago, Chile, I discovered that Walmart had purchased a majority share of D&S, one of the largest retail chains in Chile. I became fascinated with the development of Walmart in Chile. Foreign, big-box chain stores have had limited success in Chile. JCPenney, Sears, Home Depot, and Carrefour have all failed.[5] I was interested in seeing how Walmart would do. Chile also provides an interesting example, because, since the 1973 overthrow of Salvador Allende, a democratically elected Socialist president, Chile has pursued a neoliberal, free-market approach including vast privatization, export-led development, and opening up to foreign investment. Chile has been hailed

---

5. JCPenney and Carrefour survived for five years, Home Depot for four. Ultimately, national Chilean companies bought out all of these stores. Part of the problem for these global companies is that retailing in Chile is extremely competitive in a relatively small market (population 16,000,000). Another problem is the credit system. Most major retailers in Chile have their own credit cards and banks that generously add to their profitability. The situation for Walmart is different, because they bought out a national chain.

as Latin America's "free-market miracle." Under these economic conditions, it would seem that the Walmart model had the potential to flourish.

In 2011, I returned to Chile on a Fulbright for seven months to understand Walmart's impact. I was originally interested in the role of Peruvian immigrants in the retail industry, but once I arrived in Santiago and connected with the UFCW, I became increasingly interested in the relationship between Chilean unions and Walmart. Since there are no unions to represent Walmart workers in the United States, it was especially interesting to observe how workers at unionized Walmart stores and warehouses in Chile were faring.

I made various strategic choices in designing the methodology for this project. I decided that I was not interested in interviewing Walmart management. Unlike my previous work (Bank Muñoz 2008) in which I spent significant time interviewing management, in this project I really wanted to focus on workers and their unions. I made this decision because there is a well-established literature on the Walmart business model that I did not feel needed repeating.

I was first able to gain access to Walmart unions in Chile through a contact in the UFCW in the United States. After I made the initial contact and had a better sense of the lay of the land, I made contacts with two retail federations and seven unions. I also felt strongly about interviewing suppliers for Walmart in Chile. This proved to be a very difficult task, since most suppliers were nervous or scared about revealing too much information about their relationships with Walmart. I was able to make contact with two suppliers, and from there I was able to use snowball sampling to gain access to eight more suppliers.

In short, I conducted seven months of ethnographic fieldwork in Chile from December 2010 to July 2011. During the course of the seven months I conducted in-depth interviews with a total of forty-five participants: ten Walmart suppliers, five union presidents, seven union leaders, the head of the small business association, two union lawyers, and twenty Walmart workers. Follow up interviews occurred from 2012–2015 during shorter visits to Chile. Pseudonyms are used for many of the participants, however some of them wanted me to use their real names. Therefore there is a mix of pseudonyms and real names throughout the book. In addition, I was a participant observer at weekly union meetings, union rallies, and quarterly union membership meetings. I also spent a significant amount of time going to different Walmart stores and warehouses and observing the workplace environment. I was able to obtain secondary data from unions, the Chilean Ministry of Labor, and Walmart's website. In addition, I have a collection of Chilean and U.S. newspaper articles on Walmart in Chile.

As with all social science research, the methodological choices I made in this process led to limitations in the data. I didn't interview a random sample of Walmart workers. I interviewed union activists and union leaders. I didn't interview representatives of all eighty-two Walmart unions, because I was most interested in unions that were engaged in actual organizing. I have attempted to correct for some of the limitations through participant observation. Participating on a daily and weekly basis with various unions gave me insights that I would not have been privy to by only conducting in-depth interviews. In all, I attended about twenty union meetings and two union assemblies.

This project is both an academic study and an organizing project; it is not a value-neutral project. I was not only interested in learning about how Chilean unions are dealing with Walmart, I was also interested in participating in their efforts. And workers, union leaders, and community organizations were all interested in developing and deepening their practices. They wanted to learn about the U.S. labor movement, just as much as I wanted to learn about their struggles. The result was to slowly build transnational ties between the U.S. labor movement and the Chilean labor movement.

As a U.S. academic, opportunities to build transnational labor solidarity do not come knocking at my door frequently. I am grateful to have the opportunity to be working with incredible people in both the Chilean and U.S. labor movements. However, building these bridges is not always easy or straightforward. During my time in Chile, there were concerns on the Chilean side about how much to trust U.S. unions. On the U.S. side, the organizations I was working with wanted to know how representative of all Walmart workers the independent unions were, and how serious they were about fighting Walmart. Those dynamics put me right in the middle. As a Chilean I felt loyal to the unions I had relationships with. I wanted to make sure that I wasn't overstepping my role in trying to make these connections. I wanted to make sure they would be able to remain autonomous. There are far too many examples in transnational organizing of U.S. unions assuming they had all the right answers. This kind of arrogance has hurt more than one campaign. Conversely, I have deeper relationships with the U.S. labor movement. I did not want them to put their scarce resources into Chilean unions that liked giving a good speech but weren't going to do more than that. In short, I wanted and needed to be seen as legitimate to both sides. The people one works with in each organization make a huge difference in terms of relationship building. Fortunately, the Americans I was working with from the UFCW and Change-to-Win were respectful and interested in learning from the Chilean unions. They did not arrogantly assume they had all the right answers. They were interested in building a long-term relationship. The Chilean unions were equally interested in learning from their U.S. counterparts. They set aside some of their preconceived notions about "Americans" and opened up to me as a researcher and to the unions. Of course, no relationships are free of tensions or disagreements—this is also true for these actors.

Overview of the Book

In chapter 2, I lay out the importance of institutional context in Walmart's global expansion. Walmart has not effectively been able to replicate its model wholesale across countries and continents. It has had to adapt to culture, politics, and regulatory climate. In this chapter, I explore the Chilean labor movement and labor code and explain their role in Walmart's particular model in Chile. I draw comparisons to Walmart in the United States and Walmart's other global operations.

In Chapter 3, I present the analytical framework for the book. I argue that the warehouse union can be characterized by what I call *strategic democracy*, whereas the retail unions are characterized by *flexible militancy*. The warehouse workers have significant structural power, a tradition of political education, leaders with trade union experience, and a deeper culture of union democracy. As a result they have been particularly successful in achieving economic gains. The retail workers are newer unions with weaker social power but a strong culture of autonomy and militancy, and democratic structures. They have achieved some economic gains and have significantly and effectively challenged Walmart culture. These two models of unionism set up the case studies in chapters 4 and 5.

Chapter 4 looks at the warehouse union in detail. Here I explore workplace abuses, organizing strategy, and outcomes. Here I give life to the conceptual framework in chapter 3 by illustrating how the warehouse union engages in strategic democracy and looking at concrete at outcomes. At the heart of their success is a strategy that creates conditions for workers to control the productive process and have significant leverage vis-à-vis Walmart.

In chapter 5 I discuss the retail unions in detail. Again I look at workplace abuses, organizing strategy, and outcomes for these unions. The retail unions are complex and multifaceted particularly because they represent over 4,000 workers. Although the two retail federations differ in their cultures and strategies, both can still be characterized by flexible militancy. Their structural location, expansive geography, on the ground flexibility, and militancy shape their outcomes.

In chapter 6, I draw conclusions from the case study in Chile. I also move to thinking about the global implications of the Chilean case, in particular, thinking through the challenges and opportunities for global solidarity.

2

WALMART IN CHILE

Walmart had many reasons to be interested in Chile. The country is known for its stable and friendly business environment and has experienced rapid growth in the retail industry. Furthermore, in the acquisition of D&S, Walmart would attain the Presto credit card, which would add value to the company. But to really understand what made Chile a model country for Walmart we must first understand some Chilean context and history.

Chile's Road to Neoliberalism

On September 11, 1973, the Chilean military, with encouragement and support from the United States under Richard Nixon's administration, executed a brutal coup d'état against the democratically elected, socialist president Salvador Allende. Chile was not alone in this upheaval, as there was widespread instability in the Southern Cone. The 1960s and 1970s saw a wave of coups that included Brazil (1964–85), Argentina

(1976–83), Uruguay (1973–84), Bolivia (several between 1964 and 1982), Ecuador (several between 1960 and 1979), Paraguay (1954–89), and Peru (1968–75) (Drake 1996; Martínez and Díaz 1996).

At the time of the coup in Chile, only thirty-six Allende supporters remained inside the national palace (La Moneda) during Allende's last speech, yet the military still found it necessary to launch twenty-four rockets into the palace (Klein 2008). Practically overnight, the coup transformed one of the most historically democratic and stable societies in Latin America into one of the most repressive and undemocratic ones (Drake 1996). Chile became a testing ground for neoliberalism.

Salvador Allende was one of the first democratically elected Marxist presidents in Latin America. He narrowly won the 1970 election against Jorge Alessandri, an independent supported by the Chilean right. Most important, Allende did not win a majority of the vote. He won 36.3 percent of the vote, while Alessandri, representing the right wing, took 34.9 percent, and the Christian Democratic candidate, Radomiro Tomic, took 27.8 percent (Angell 1972). This split would make it very difficult to implement the program Allende had in mind. Nonetheless, upon taking office Allende began to implement his economic program which included nationalizing copper as well as other key industries (Winn 1986), government administration of the health and education systems, land seizure and redistribution, and agrarian reform (which was already underway by the policies of former president Eduardo Frei). One of the first things Allende did was to raise the real wages of blue-collar workers by 37 to 41 percent and white-collar workers by 8 to 10 percent (Dornbusch and Edwards 1992; Stallings 1978) while simultaneously freezing prices. As a result of these policies, in 1971 the Chilean economy grew substantially, while unemployment dropped to under 4 percent. During 1971 the economy grew a substantial 9 percent, and unemployment dropped by more than half to 4 percent. Furthermore, the Allende government also nationalized all but three of Chile's largest banks (Collins and Lear 1995).

Perhaps most contentious was Allende's "Social and Mixed Areas" program. Under the Allende administration, companies were divided into government-owned/run, mixed firms that were public and private partnerships, and privately held firms (Stallings 1978). Firms with capital exceeding over a million U.S. dollars would be put into the social and mixed areas. This angered both the left and the right. The bourgeois sectors of the economy were furious to see their industries taken over, despite being paid for them. Conversely, many factory workers were angry that their workplaces were not being taken over or did not make the government's list of ninety-one firms that were going to be incorporated into the social and mixed areas in early 1972 (Armstrong and Águila 2006; Stallings 1978; Winn 1986). By 1973 the state owned over 250 firms and had intervened in an additional 259 (Martínez and Díaz 1996).

By late 1972 Allende had lost control of the congress and there were increasing political challenges rising from the right wing, middle class, and small business communities. Manufacturers objected to fixed prices and stopped producing. The right wing elites in Chile staged their first strike in October 1972 when the truck owners association blocked roads leading to Santiago and were quickly joined by the retail merchants association (Tinsman 2014). This event created a crisis and food shortage. The left and workers responded by calling for the rapid nationalization of distribution firms, retail chains, and transportation. In turmoil, the government floundered and brought in the military (Stallings 1978). Meanwhile, the gross domestic product dropped to 5.6 percent and there was increasing social unrest and intervention from U.S. corporations and the Central Intelligence Agency (CIA). By 1972 inflation, which had been at an all-time low when Allende took office, skyrocketed to 140 percent (Collins and Lear 1995; Constable and Valenzuela 1991).

The history and critiques of Allende's presidency are too lengthy to detail here.[1] Clearly Allende posed a major threat to the United States and its Cold War policies. The United States was not going to let the world witness a successful democratic-socialist experiment. The well-documented history of the coup and recently released CIA documents show the depth of U.S. involvement in the coup (Collins and Lear 1995; Constable and Valenzuela 1991; Harvey 2005; Klein 2008; Kornbluh 2003; Verdugo 2003). In short, the coup and the massive societal changes that came with it inextricably linked the United States and Chile. The changes that Allende brought about continue to form the basis of expectations and goals of many contemporary union members, certainly those whom I have been

---

1. There are many good sources that the reader can look at for history (Boorstein 1977; Harmer 2014; Qureshi 2008).

working with. They continue to resist the revanchist policies of his successor, Augusto Pinochet.

During the seventeen-year dictatorship of Augusto Pinochet, Chile served as the testing ground for the neoliberal state. Immediately after the coup, as advised by U.S. economist Milton Friedman and the "Chicago Boys,"[2] Pinochet essentially undid all of the work of the Allende and Frei governments. He cut taxes, liberalized trade, privatized health care, social security, and education (creating a system of vouchers and charter schools), cut social spending, and deregulated the banking system (Harvey 2005; Klein 2008; Martínez and Díaz 1996). The economic "shock treatment" offered by Friedman and others created a template for neoliberal interventions across the globe (Klein 2008). Sergio DeCastro, Pinochet's finance minister, cut spending by 27 percent in 1975. This drastic reduction sent the Chilean economy into a tailspin. Chile lost 177,000 jobs between 1973 and 1983 (Klein 2008). Its unemployment levels, which were only about 3 percent during Allende's administration, reached over 20 percent by 1978 (Constable and Valenzuela 1991; Martínez and Díaz 1996).

The abrupt shift from an import-substitution model that relied on a closed economy and protectionism to an export-oriented economy created a series of crises, and in 1982 the free market experiment crashed and burned when Chile's economy collapsed (Drake 1996; Martínez and Díaz 1996). In the early 1980s even employers who had backed the military coup were having regrets. For example, when Pinochet returned state-owned textile factories back to private owners, the owners assumed that they would receive the same level of government protection they had before Allende. However, under Pinochet's export-oriented economy, they were forced to compete in the global marketplace. As a result many textile mills closed or had to reinvent themselves (Winn 2004). Furthermore, debt exploded, inflation reached over 120 percent, and unemployment hit 30 percent (Klein 2008). The primary reason for the collapse was the deregulation of the banking industry, which bought up the country's assets

---

2. The "Chicago Boys" were a group of Chilean economists mostly trained at the University of Chicago under Milton Friedman. Many of them returned to Chile and affiliated with the Catholic University and trained others in Friedman's extremist free-market model. The original group of Chicago Boys received a free education financed by the Ford Foundation, under the U.S. government's "Chile Project" (Klein 2008).

and incurred a debt of $14 billion (Klein 2008; Winn 2004). Collins and Lear wrote that, "The government intervened massively in the financial sector. Over the next two years, the government absorbed the debts of many large businesses, restoring them to soundness before selling them off to private interests. . . . By contrast, middle class families watched with disbelief and anger as the balances on their home mortgages, indexed to the dollar value of the peso, soared; but the government offered them no relief" (1995, 33).[3]

The 1982 collapse of the Chilean economy was so deep and so hopeless that in an ironic twist, Pinochet had to rely on some of Allende's socialist practices and was forced to renationalize some industries (Martínez and Díaz 1996). As Klein eloquently argues, "Chile under Pinochet and the Chicago boys was not a capitalist state featuring a liberated market but a corporatist one. What Chile pioneered under Pinochet was an evolution of corporatism: a mutually supporting alliance between a police state and large corporations, joining forces to wage all-out war on the third power sector—the workers—thereby drastically increasing the alliance's share of the national wealth" (2008: 105). There is essentially nothing about the "free market" that explains the so-called Chilean economic miracle. At every step of the way there was some level of state or corporate intervention.

Neoliberalism and the Return to Democracy

In 1988 Chile held a referendum on whether or not to continue with eight more years of military dictatorship. Pinochet lost the referendum in a 56 percent to 44 percent vote (Martínez and Díaz 1996). Elections were scheduled for the following year, and Patricio Aylwin of the center-left coalition (La Concertación) overwhelmingly won the election. La Concertación remained in power (albeit with different presidents) until January 2010, when right-wing candidate Sebastián Piñera won the national election. In 2014, La Nueva Mayoría, a center-left coalition similar to the Concertación, won the election under the leadership of Michelle Bachelet.

---

3. This event strikingly resembles President George W. Bush's (signed by President Barack Obama) bailout of the U.S. financial industry in 2008, which saved Wall Street but did nothing to protect working and middle class homeowners.

In response to student protests and other social movements, the coalition ran on three main issues, free access to higher education within six years, constitutional reform, and fiscal reform (Gaudichaud 2015).

The election of Aylwin and the Concertación marked the transition to democracy in Chile; however, the Concertación initially made no fundamental changes to law. This inaction was because it was a transition government that feared that implementing too many social policies could rock the boat, and also because members of La Concertación both intellectually and practically supported some of the neoliberal principles that had been implemented (Frank 2004).

Although the Concertación eventually did make some changes to the labor code, eliminated life-time senators, and significantly expanded government spending, it has strikingly little to show for having been in power for twenty-one years (longer than the dictatorship). The Chilean economic miracle continues to rely on cheap and flexible labor and minimal regulation (Moulian 2002; Winn 2004).

Inequality

Chile remains an extremely unequal country. In 1990, the top 10 percent of income earners made thirty times the amount of the bottom 10 percent. By 2009 the top 10 percent earned forty-six times the amount the bottom 10 percent earned. Torche (2005) discusses extreme income inequality concentrated at the very top. Government programs can mitigate the worst aspects of inequality, even under neoliberalism but often offer only a slight improvement. The policies of the Concertación have definitely made a difference in reducing poverty, but the fact remains that Chile continues to be in the top ten of unequal countries in the world. Much more significant government intervention must exist for Chile to return to the lower levels of inequality achieved under Allende. Between 1967 and 1973 there was significant reduction in inequality. In fact, by 1973 the Gini index[4] was down to .45 (Palma 2008). By 1987, under the Pinochet regime, the Gini index peaked at .62 (Palma 2008). In 2013, the Gini index for Chile was stable at .51, making it the most unequal country in the Organization for Economic

---

4. The Gini index/coefficient is a measure of inequality, usually income or wealth. A zero on the index signifies perfect equality. A one on the scale signifies perfect inequality.

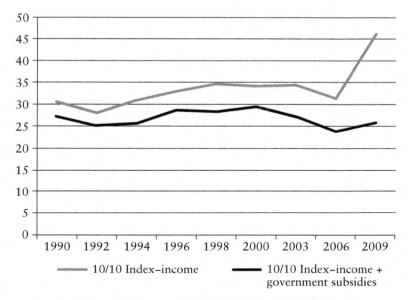

Figure 2.1. Income distribution in Chile, 1990–2009.

Definition: Index 10/10: Ratio of top 10 percent of income earners to bottom 10 percent of income earners.
Source: CASEN Survey Chile. Thanks to Florencia Torche for generating the data for 1990–2009.

Cooperation and Development (OECD 2013). This number is especially significant in a period where worker productivity has increased by nearly 90 percent, while real wages have increased only 20 percent (Gaudichaud 2015).

The Consumer Society

Besides economic changes, the neoliberal project has fundamentally changed Chilean society and culture. Angell (1972) for example, argues that pre-1973 Chile as a society expected and demanded benefits and accountability from its government. It was widely viewed as one of the most democratic and participatory societies in Latin America (Drake 1996; Stallings 1978; Valenzuela 1976). It was a society that valued collectivity as opposed to the individual (Araujo and Martuccelli 2012; Moulian 2002). Chile did experience a cultural shift in a number of different ways.

First, and perhaps foremost, the brutal nature of the dictatorship disincentivized political action in any form. Citizens who might have been involved in political work often cautioned their children to stay away from politics, for fear that they might be arrested, detained, and tortured or killed (Martínez and Díaz 1996). It was not until the mid-1980s that widespread protest against the dictatorship became more common. As a result, a whole generation of Chilean young people learned to not talk politics or otherwise be engaged in politics. Elections provide a limited but useful example of this social transformation. In the 1988 Chilean national plebiscite, which determined whether Pinochet would extend his rule by eight years, over 97 percent of the population voted, and the "No" side (against the extension of Pinochet's rule) won with over 56 percent of the vote. In the 1989 constitutional referendum, which sought to transition the country to democracy, over 93 percent of the electorate turned out to vote. Similarly, the 1989 presidential election also yielded a phenomenal voter turnout with 95 percent of registered voters. However, by the 2009 presidential election only 67 percent of the eligible population had registered to vote (Instituto Nacional de Estadísticas 2011). Of course elections are not the only method of civic engagement, and we see this clearly in the 2013 election where voter turnout was at an all-time low, but social movements in the preceding years had been the largest since the dictatorship. So while neoliberalism may not have created an apathetic society, between 1995 and 2006 Chile experienced a lack of political engagement and disinvestment in politics.

Second, as a society, Chile became much more consumer oriented, especially in the transition to democracy. The expansion of access to credit during and after the dictatorship facilitated the development of malls, chain stores, and big-box stores (Stillerman 2004; Stillerman and Salcedo 2012). These retailers became a consumer's paradise. Chilean citizens earning over a meager $125 per month could apply for credit. This eligibility opened up a whole new world giving working-class and lower middle-class consumers a chance to own color TVs, microwaves, and the newest products on the market. At the same time, it offered these same populations a way to survive economic downturns, especially chronic unemployment and underemployment, under the new neoliberal order (Stillerman 2012; Van Bavel and Sell Trujillo 2003). In the postdictatorship period, Chile experienced the largest expansion of department/retail store credit in Latin America. While bank credit cards only tripled between 1993 and 2007, department store credit cards expanded nearly fifteen-fold in the same period (Ossandón 2014). It is not surprising then that consumer debt in Chile had reached nearly 4,000,000 U.S. dollars[5] by 1995, with 66 percent of the debtors coming from the working-class and lower middle-class sectors of the economy (Moulian 2002). However, between 2001 and 2008 consumer debt grew a mind-blowing 254 percent to nearly 34,000,000 U.S. dollars (Barrionuevo 2011).

People of all socioeconomic backgrounds are working more to pay off or keep up with their credit debt. In his insightful book *Chile Actual: La Anatomía de un Mito*, Moulian describes a new type of citizen: the *ciudadano credit-card* (the credit-card citizen). This citizen is controlled by credit cards and has learned that the best thing he can do is continue to be a loyal, hard-working employee, because that is what opens up the doors of credit (2002: 103). While Moulian intends to be a polemicist, there is truth to his argument. Workers saddled with debt are less likely to engage in actions that will risk their livelihoods. In Stillerman's chapter on Madeco workers, union leaders observe, "that indebted workers feel compelled to work extensive overtime on a regular basis in order to satisfy credit payments. This makes them more beholden to employers, gives them less time to participate in union activities, and makes them less willing to threaten their good relations with the boss" (2004, 181). I found the same dynamics in both the warehouse and retail unions with whom I worked. Worker activists and union leaders point to the difficulty in breaking individualism, fighting for the collective, and not going into debt (see chapter 5).

Most troubling is the use of credit for basic necessities. In my seven months in Chile I witnessed hundreds of people purchasing bread, butter, eggs, and milk using Walmart's Presto credit card at Walmart stores. This high-interest credit card does not have a grace period, so consumers are immediately paying interest on all of their purchases. Not paying one's debt then becomes a significant issue for the *ciudadano credit card* because no longer having access to credit becomes like losing your citizenship, because debtors become blacklisted for jobs, housing, private schools, and banking. Of course, amassing huge amounts of debt is not

---

5. Author calculated the exchange rate between pesos and dollars for 1995.

unique to Chileans; it is part of a new global debt culture. However, this level of debt is particularly striking in Chile, because it is such a small country and its citizens are disproportionately indebted. Credit, and the new consumer culture, poses significant challenges for Chilean society. Chilean lives become in service to their debt. This situation poses unique challenges to unions and social movements. To fully understand the context for the contemporary Chilean labor movement and in particular the success of the Walmart unions in a generally dismal labor movement, we must first understand the history and development of Chilean unions.

Labor, Political Parties, and the State: 1924–1973

Chilean workers have a long history of labor struggle and resistance. A notable early example was the Santa Maria School massacre on December 21, 1907, in which the Chilean army murdered 2,000 striking nitrate miners and their wives and children. Workers had been striking for better pay and working conditions, as the labor camps near the mines were dreadful and mine managers were despicable (Artaza Barrios 1998; Valenzuela 1976). Workers mobilized with increasing intensity throughout the early twentieth century, but no formal labor code was enacted until 1931 (Drake 1996). The labor movement at the time had mixed feelings about establishing a labor code that would force them to meet certain requirements, yet they liked the idea of formalizing their status, and the requirement of profit sharing. Elites, by contrast, had a vested interest in passing a labor code that would restrict labor. In short, while the first labor code established some rights and protections for workers, it also helped to institutionalize weak union structures (Angell 1972; Drake 1996; Valenzuela 1976).

The 1931 labor code had some key features. First, it established a system of labor legislation that specified the internal organization of unions in a very detailed way. For example, unions were not allowed to have cash on hand and had to deposit dues into a state bank and ask for authorization to withdraw funds. This regulation seriously inhibited labor's ability to go on strike, since they could not use dues money to support strikes. Second, the 1931 labor code gave the state significant control over unions through the courts and executive branch. The state also established a network of labor inspectorates that controlled unions and mediated labor conflicts. Third, many small unions dominated the labor movement and engaged in collective bargaining separately. Finally, the code separated blue-collar unions from white collar/professional unions, further fragmenting workers.

Despite these limitations, the Chilean labor movement managed to play a fundamental role in establishing Chilean democracy. Angell (1972) and Valenzuela (1976) both argue that weak union structures were at least partially responsible for the development of working-class parties that would champion workers' issues. Since the labor code did not comprehensively protect workers, they sought change through politics. As Angell (1972) points out, the Chilean labor movement was unique in Latin America for a number of reasons. First, it was representative enough of the working class to prevent the formation of an aristocracy of labor privileging a few. Second, Chilean unions have never been controlled by the state or employers, as they are in Brazil and Mexico. Finally, no single political party dominates unions; diverse and conflicting ideologies compete to win the loyalty of workers and unions. Chilean workers' relative independence from employers, the state, and political parties allowed them to develop not only class-consciousness but also political savvy.

Although one can argue that the 1931 labor code primarily benefitted elites over workers, it did have three important features that were instrumental in the growth of the union movement. First, it made unionization a right and therefore legal. This regulation had the effect of incorporating thousands of workers into the labor movement. Second, when workers organized a union, membership was compulsory for blue-collar workers. Finally, the labor code regulated working conditions and established a system of social security and minimum wages (Valenzuela 1976). Of course, the Chilean labor movement and worker protections did not include everyone. Labor was particularly strong in traditional, male-dominated sectors such as manufacturing and copper (Leiva 2013). The public sector was a mixed case, because while they weren't formally allowed to unionize, they did have strong associations that essentially acted like unions. However, agricultural and domestic workers were largely excluded from the traditional labor movement and labor policy. Inroads in representing these workers were just starting when the coup took place.

Between 1970 and 1973, workers made unprecedented gains in wages, working conditions, and job stability, and by 1973, 35 percent of the

Chilean workforce was unionized (Collins and Lear 1995). Before the dictatorship, organized workers had strong political ties and regularly participated in "national debates over questions of employment and social policy, regularly defending the unorganized majority of urban workers. . . . Unions were fundamental vehicles for widening participation in the political process and making economic development more equitable" (Collins and Lear 1995, 69).

The election of Salvador Allende in 1970 and the promise of democratic socialism gave the labor movement unprecedented leverage. One noteworthy example of this newfound power was the 1971 worker takeover of the largest textile mill in Chile, Fábrica Yarur. As Winn (1986) argues, this case was unique because the takeover happened with the factory owners on site. The takeover pushed a reluctant Allende government to socialize the mill, propelling the socialist experiment forward (Winn 1986). Winn states, "to Chile's workers, peasants and pobladores, the election of a 'Popular Government' was a signal for them to take the revolution into their own hands and fulfill their historic aspirations through direct action from below" (1986, 140). Being the very first workers to do this, the Yarur workers led the way in socialism from below, encouraging other workers into action. Unfortunately, the many experiments in socialism from below that occurred in this period, from factory takeovers to land seizures, were short lived as the country entered economic crisis in 1972 followed by the coup in 1973.

Labor Code Reform: 1973–1989

Pinochet and the military attacked workers and union leaders with special vengeance in the days after the coup, according to a report by the International Labor Organization (ILO): "In the aftermath of the coup, 2,200 union leaders were fired, 110 were killed, and 230 were jailed" (cited in Collins and Lear 1995, 70). Between 1973 and 1978 nearly all labor rights for both unionized and unorganized workers were suspended. Health and safety were deregulated as the government destroyed the landmark law of Occupational Health and Accidents. In 1979 Pinochet and his advisers rolled out a new labor code. The 1979 Labor Code followed the neoliberal model, creating a system that allowed employers to organize their workplaces as they saw fit. This reorganization often included union busting: "The new Labor Code facilitated shifting workers from one position to another within a firm, and more importantly allowed employers to fire workers at will, individually or *en masse,* for 'business necessities'" (Collins and Lear 1995, 76; see also Armstrong and Águila 2006). These changes were unprecedented in Chilean history (Palacios-Valladares 2011); in fact, in many industrialized nations (outside of the United States where employer flexibility has nearly always been a given) the labor code protects workers against arbitrary firing.

Furthermore, the new labor code placed restrictions on who could unionize, while eliminating the distinction between white-collar and blue-collar workers (Armstrong and Águila 2006). Only workers employed for at least six consecutive months were eligible to unionize. This rule excluded seasonal and temporary workers and the vast majority of workers in the informal labor market (Collins and Lear 1995). It also placed major restrictions on organizing and transformed the labor movement from a mixed model where industrial and enterprise unions could coexist—as in the United States where whole sectors of the economy are organized by one union (for example, auto manufacturing), as well as in local unions that organize on a shopfloor level—to an exclusive enterprise model where each workplace has its own union (Armstrong and Águila 2006). In addition, the Pinochet labor code eliminated compulsory union membership and allowed a single workplace to have multiple unions.

There is a spirited debate in labor studies about the costs and benefits of exclusive representation. Under U.S. labor law, unionized workplaces are exclusively represented by one union. In other words, employers cannot bargain with more than one union. However, other countries, such as the United Kingdom, France, Japan, and Chile, allow multiple unions or workplace associations within one workplace. Some scholars argue that allowing multiple unions increases the potential for democracy (Dimick 2010), because it forces the different organizations to compete with each other, thereby reducing bureaucracy. Dimick (2010) argues that one of the reasons that U.S. unions are less democratic than UK unions is because they have exclusive representation and therefore spend time and money building up bureaucratic structures. In the United Kingdom, unions compete with each other for the lowest dues and best contracts, minimizing bureaucracy. However, other scholars argue that the lack of exclusive representation fragments unions, making it difficult to effectively fight the employer (Armstrong and Águila 2006; Durán and Kremerman 2015; Reid and Kurth 1984). In Chile, this policy has both positive and negative repercussions. On the one hand, the open-shop model has allowed for workers to organize militant and democratic unions, even in a shop with a corrupt union. On the other hand, it keeps stores largely fragmented, which makes cross-sector organizing difficult. For example, at Híper Líder Santa Amalia, a Walmart Supercenter in Santiago, the yellow union[6] represents about 30 percent of workers, the autonomous independent union represents 60 percent of workers, and another independent union represents 10 percent of workers. These three different unions negotiate contracts at different times and have variable representation. Furthermore, the policy of nonexclusive representation makes strikebreaking easier, because one union might vote to go on strike, and the workers represented by the other unions might cross the picket line.

Under the Pinochet-era labor code, even when workers were able to bargain collectively, they were restricted to the issue of wages. No other labor issues, such as health and safety or breaks, were subject to collective bargaining (Barrera and Valenzuela 1987). Even within the issue of wages, workers had no guarantees. An amendment to the labor code allowed that wages could be negotiated downward, rather than keeping up with inflation at a minimum. Therefore when unions tried to collectively bargain over wages, employers would more often than not start at zero, rather than the wages in the last contract.

Finally, Pinochet's labor code changed the nature of strikes. Where strikes had once been a significant source of worker power, strikes under the new labor code were generally ineffective. Employers were now able to lock workers out, hire replacement workers, and negotiate individually with striking workers. Additionally, a strike was considered legal only if no contract had been signed and if a majority of union members supported it. Strikes could only take place in one factory or shop at a time and were limited to a two-month period. Meanwhile, skyrocketing

---

6. "Yellow union" is a term for a corrupt or company union whose interests are aligned with the employer over the workers.

unemployment gave employers even more leverage to break strikes (Armstrong and Águila 2006; Collins and Lear 1995).

By 1987, union membership accounted for a mere 11 percent of the workforce (Collins and Lear 1995). In the transition to democracy the labor movement recovered somewhat, reaching 19 percent union density in 1991, but falling to 13 percent in 1999 (Durán and Kremerman 2015; Volker 2004). In other words, for most of the years that the Concertación has been in power union density has gone down or remained flat. This stagnation is at least in part because the Concertación governments have not significantly reformed the labor code. In 2009, after twenty years of democratic rule, union density was only 14.3 percent (OECD 2015). In 2013, the density ratio was essentially the same, at 14.2 percent (Dirección de Trabajo 2014). It is important to note that nearly 50 percent of large firms are unionized, but only 4.5 percent of small firms have unions. Furthermore, nearly 70 percent of Chilean workers are employed by firms with fewer than eight employees, the minimum number needed to form a union. Thus a large part of the workforce is completely excluded from labor unions (Gaudichaud 2015). The Chilean labor movement is indeed very far from the 34 percent union density it had achieved in 1973.

Despite the brutal labor environment produced by the dictatorship, workers did continue to organize and agitate during this period. Contrary to many analysts of contentious politics, Stillerman (1998) argues that while extremely repressive, the Pinochet dictatorship in Chile also offered workers different political opportunities, at least early on. He states, "labor policy is often highly sensitive, because the dictatorship must balance its desire to control labor with its need to win workers' consent if the economy is to function at all" (Stillerman 1998, 100). In other words, the dictatorship needed to balance despotism and consent, and in that it created political opportunities for union leaders and workers.

Stillerman's case study of Madeco, the Chilean metal workers union, illustrates this particular union's complex trajectory. Madeco was one of the strongest, most organized unions in Chile during the Allende period. Stillerman divides his case into three periods, 1973–78, 1978–82, and 1983–89. He finds that a cycle of "clandestinity-radicalism-demobilization" (1998, 104) explains the union's trajectory better than demise as a result of the coup. Severe repression marked the first period, characterized by "clandestine unionism." For example, Madeco's new personnel manager sent "270 Madeco workers identified with the UP [Unidad Popular] government to the National Stadium where military officials interrogated, tortured, and imprisoned them" (Stillerman 1998, 116). At the same time, Pinochet and his advisers could not come to an agreement about labor-law reform; technically, the old labor code remained on the books, giving workers the opportunity to organize clandestinely and slow down the changes to their working conditions. For example, even though during this period there was a dramatic workforce reduction (nearly 50 percent of workers were laid off), managers couldn't simply fire non-leftist workers without cause, and they had to pay significant severance packages, per the labor code. Stillerman (1998) insightfully articulates that the regime's paralysis regarding labor law and their legalistic ideology essentially gave workers the power to negotiate their dismissals.

Furthermore, Stillerman argues that the repression forced a new generation of workers into clandestine organizing. Covert organizing eventually led to open resistance on the shop floor. The new labor code, the 1978 Plan Laboral (Labor Law), and the 1982 economic crisis further catalyzed workers' discontent and created the conditions for the 1983 strike. The fact that Madeco held a two-month strike in the middle of the dictatorship is a testament to the kind of organizing and militancy that were happening at the same time as severe repression. The Madeco story illustrates that the dictatorship was not able to destroy labor militancy at a local level, even though it effectively destroyed the national labor movement.

Perhaps most important, Stillerman's case study of Madeco explains how the Chilean labor movement was able to play an instrumental role in fueling the social movement that toppled Pinochet and pushed forward democratization despite severe repression. In April 1983, the Confederation of Copper Workers called a national strike against the regime. These "days of protest" occurred at the beginning of each month for the remainder of 1983 and a few months in 1984 (Martínez and Díaz 1996). These protests brought in broader coalitions and reduced fear. In the early part of the dictatorship protests were carried out by small groups of mostly militant leftists, many of whom paid with their lives. However, when the most powerful, and arguably most important, industry union called for a national day of action, it was able to draw in the middle class and other segments of the labor movement. They were able to break what Martínez and Díaz (1996) call "heroic syndrome." Regular civilians would be protected by the sheer power of the industry and their numbers. Therefore, 1983–84 marked a turning point in the dictatorship; it was the moment in which the dictatorship started losing control of the citizenry. The labor movement once again rose to the occasion and played a decisive role working on the "No" vote in preparation for the 1988 plebiscite (Frank 2004).

The Mainstream Labor Movement: 1990–2016

Despite the labor movement's key role in Chile's return to democracy and President Aylwin's promise of a new industrial relations system, the Concertación initially made no changes to the labor code (Frank 2004, 2015). The weak labor movement had little choice but to give the government time. The Concertación relied heavily on a strategy of consensus. Although consensus can be a good thing for democracy, in the case of Chile it only helped to maintain a neoliberal status quo. A key component of the Concertación's consensus building was to remodel the industrial relations system in terms of labor-management partnership through what it called the "Acuerdo Marco." The government essentially agreed to promote negotiations between labor and management but not intervene in their affairs. In actuality this agreement gave employers legitimacy for participating in negotiations, while workers increasingly lost on key issues (Frank 2004, 2015).

Probably the most significant gain for labor under Aylwin was his restoration of "just cause" back into the labor code. Employers could no longer simply fire workers at will; they had to justify each dismissal and provide up to eleven months of severance pay (compared with a cap of five months under the 1978 Plan Laboral) (Frank 2004). On the employer side, the most significant benefit was a new collective bargaining law, which allowed only plant-level collective bargaining and excluded the public sector. Most important, "According to the new law, if this offer [employer's last offer] included a) identical stipulations as those of the old contract and b) a wage readjustment of at least the inflation level, the employer had the right to replace striking workers from the first day" (Frank 2004, 79).

Labor did not fare much better under the second Concertación government of Eduardo Freí. The labor movement expressed hopefulness of things to come when after three days in office Freí announced that public sector associations would be recognized as unions. A year later they were given collective bargaining rights (Frank 2004). The Freí administration proposed more progressive modifications to Aylwin's labor reforms, but unfortunately these were rejected by the Chilean Congress.

In the early 2000s, under Ricardo Lagos, the Concertación once again took up labor code reform. Once again, the reform did not address one of the most crucial issues for workers, sectoral bargaining, but some modest changes were implemented. For example, the Concertación established unemployment insurance, reduced the workweek from forty-eight to forty-five hours, guaranteed nondiscrimination, and granted workers some protections against arbitrary firing (Palacios-Valladares 2011). Part-time workers gained the same benefits as full-time workers in terms of pay, minimum pay, social security, holidays, and safety. Furthermore, if a labor court decided in favor of a worker who had been fired, she would have to be reinstated (Frank 2004).

Despite these improvements, the Concertación failed to halt the expansion of precarious and temporary employment facilitated by the dictatorship. The 2007 subcontracting law in Chile attempted to impose some restrictions, but it has largely failed to protect temporary and subcontracted workers. Echeverría (2010) shows that between 30 to 50 percent of firms rely on subcontracting regularly.

During Bachelet's campaign for a second term in 2013, she promised a substantial labor law reform that would "level the playing field" and eliminate the worst of the Pinochet-era Plan Laboral. However, most labor law analysts agree that while the proposed legislation makes some interesting changes, by and large it will undermine labor and significantly favor employers. For example, the proposed legislation eliminates strike breaking, while at the same time proposing that before a union and an employer can begin the collective bargaining process they must negotiate "minimal services" in case of a strike. Generally, this concept applies only to unions in strategic sectors of the economy that would have an impact on citizens, for example, hospitals, transit, and schools. However, Bachelet's legislation extends this idea to all unions. This regulation effectively weakens the impact of a strike, since the main functions of the company will remain in effect. Strikebreakers become irrelevant, since striking workers would be forced to work (No Al Plan Laboral 2016; Ugarte and Gamonal 2015). What's worse is that the ILO has sanctioned these clauses, against its own historical practice (Vergara 2016). Ultimately, the proposed labor law reform, which as of 2016 has not yet been implemented, does not address the most detrimental provisions of the Pinochet-era labor code, such as enterprise level unionism.

The mainstream[7] Chilean labor movement, represented by the Central Unitaria de Trabajadores (CUT), a parallel organization to the AFL-CIO in the United States, continues to rely on political parties to take care of labor policy. This phenomenon is relatively common in countries that have experienced dictatorships. Examples range from Brazil to South Africa, where unions have helped bring down dictatorships or bring in democracy and are then closely allied to the new ruling party and have a hard time establishing autonomy. As such, the CUT has not built a strong mass base with which it can make demands. In fact, it has done the opposite, alienating itself from local unions. This alienation is a result of the dictatorship's abolishment of the CUT and the long and difficult process it took to reestablish the organization, as well as the political calculations of the different political parties. Unfortunately, this failure has meant a flat union density (around 14 percent) and, more important, limited mobilization and membership participation. Furthermore, since the 1990s unions have been much more willing to negotiate agreements without the right to strike than to participate in collective bargaining (Frank 2015). In addition, the mainstream labor movement has been mired in infighting. None of the emerging coalitions has addressed fundamental problems with Chile's labor and political system. Most important, the CUT, remained silent on the retrograde 2016 labor law reform until it was too late to do anything about it (Vergara 2016). Of course, Chile's labor woes do not all fall squarely on the shoulders of the CUT; the Concertación

---

7. I use the term "mainstream labor movement" as the formal representatives of workers on a national level. The CUT therefore acts very much like the AFL-CIO does in the United States. This formal representation of workers does not include independent/autonomous unions or other types of workers' organizations, such as worker centers. In Chile the CUT is traditional in that it mostly represents manufacturing and core industries such as mining. It is therefore removed from issues related to the rise in women's labor market participation and suffers from a particularly androcentric perspective.

governments did little to advance labor's cause, and employers have become increasingly powerful and intransigent. Nonetheless, the CUT has steered the labor movement towards a top-down approach rather than a grassroots democracy. As a result of its downward trajectory the CUT is widely criticized by labor union leaders (Urrutia 2015).

Leiva (2012, 2013) has argued that the problem with the mainstream Chilean labor movement is that it follows an outmoded "socio-cultural matrix" characterized by five components. First, the social base of the Chilean labor movement has been rooted in the mining and urban manufacturing sectors. Second, the movement has traditionally been masculinist and androcentric. Third, the movement sees its principal obligation as defending the rights of workers through collective bargaining. Fourth, a state-centered labor movement where workers and their organizations push their demands, but the political parties and system are in charge of implementation. Finally, the mainstream movement has legitimized activism for the purposes of political pressure through the established party system, but not "through direct, autonomous, social representation . . . that arose in militant workplaces under Allende" (Leiva 2012, 109). The CUT has largely been blind to the present-day's unprecedented female labor market participation, subcontracting, flexible work arrangements, and an explosion of jobs in nontraditional sectors such as service (Leiva 2012, 2013). Although it is possible that Leiva (2012) somewhat overstates the importance of manufacturing and mining to the labor movement, since others have pointed to the longstanding significance of the public and private sectors to labor (Angell 1972; Armstrong 2006; Drake 1996), his overall point about needing a new framework for the labor movement in the twenty-first century is on point. In order for the labor movement in Chile to thrive it must incorporate new workers and reflect the country's current workforce realities.

Leiva's (2012) ideas ring true in the case of Walmart in Chile, an industry that is concentrated in the service sector, relies on "flexibility," and increasingly employs mostly women. It is not surprising that the Walmart unions I worked with were deeply suspicious of the CUT and its ties to political parties. Experienced unionists understood that this strategy had failed. Frank (2015) argues that the Pinochet regime decoupled labor from political parties, forcing unions to rely on their own strategies and ideas. Paradoxically, this attempt to weaken labor created stronger local organization. It is not entirely surprising then that the Walmart unions I worked with valued their autonomy from both the CUT and political parties. These unions align themselves much more with the alternative labor movement than the mainstream labor movement.

Alternative/Independent Labor Movement

Unlike the mainstream labor movement, which is largely stagnant, the alternative or independent labor movement in Chile is thriving. Leiva (2013) convincingly shows us that as the CUT has become more irrelevant, grassroots labor mobilizations have been on the rise. In 2006–7 a progressive labor movement seeking to be more democratic and less bureaucratic re-emerged. Of particular importance were the 25,000 subcontracted copper workers, the forestry workers, and workers in the salmon fisheries who all participated in strikes. These were all workers largely excluded from labor law. Furthermore, between 2011 and 2014, the port workers, who are not legally able to unionize, carried out a series of strikes culminating in a Unión Portuaria. The organization is not legal, but it is nonetheless extraordinarily powerful (Gaudichaud 2015).

Leiva (2013) also demonstrates that workers have been a central force in other social conflicts, such as the student movement, environmental movement, and the indigenous rights movement. Further, Leiva shows that labor's participation in labor and other social movement mobilizations has been driven at the local level, with the CUT playing a minimal role in these mobilizations. Using a chronology developed by the Observatorio Social de América Latina-Social Observatory of Latin America (OSAL), Leiva shows that between 2007 and 2014 unions and federations were responsible for 389 mobilizations, while the CUT was responsible for only eighteen, primarily organizing May Day marches. Additionally, Armstrong and Águila's (2011) show that in 2009, 22,000 workers went on legal strikes, whereas over 1.5 million workers participated in illegal strikes. Interestingly, illegal strikes are more common in Chile's provinces than in the Metropolitan district.[8] Pérez (2014) shows that in eight of the

---

8. Until 2007 Chile was divided into thirteen different provinces called *regiones*. Since then, the addition of two new *regiones* has brought the total to fifteen.

twelve regional districts there were more illegal than legal strikes. For example, in Region V (Valparaiso) and Region X (Los Lagos) over 67 percent of strikes between 1990 and 2009 were illegal. In Regions XI (Aysén) and XII (Magallanes) over 77 percent of strikes during the same period were illegal. By contrast, only 28 percent of strikes in the Metropolitan District were illegal (Pérez 2014).

Furthermore, the industries with the greatest participation in illegal strikes between 1990 and 2009 were government[9] (central, regional, and municipal)—98.5 percent; health (public and private)—85.6 percent; electricity, water, and sanitation—77 percent; construction—75 percent; and transport and communications—69 percent. By contrast, the industries with the greatest percentage of strikes sanctioned by Chilean labor law were commerce/retail—82.6 percent; manufacturing—82.5 percent; and banking/financial services—79.4 percent (Pérez 2014). It is not surprising then that with the exception of commerce, legal strikes are occurring in industries that have been traditional union strongholds and in the metropolitan region. Illegal strikes, with the exception of transportation, are taking place in industries historically excluded from the labor code and outside of the metropolitan region.

Still, while the distribution of legal and illegal strikes has changed, overall strikes have gone down significantly since the Allende period. For example, in 1970 nearly 2,000,000 workers participated in legal and illegal strikes, and in 1973, before the coup, over 900,000 workers had participated in strikes. By contrast, in 1991 only about 350,000 workers had participated in a strike, and by 2002 the figure had reached only 430,000 (Armstrong and Águila 2006).

On the whole, the Chilean labor movement has experienced great decline since the dictatorship. At its peak in 1973, 34 percent of Chilean workers were unionized; by 1987 this number had drastically dropped to 11 percent, and today it hovers around 15 percent. However, we should understand the decline in a nuanced way. Both Stillerman (1998) and Leiva (2013) provide good counterexamples to the narrative of neoliberalism. Although there is no question that the Plan Laboral and an

---

9. Public sector workers in Chile do not have the right to strike under the labor code, therefore all strikes in this industry are inherently illegal strikes. This explains the high number for both government workers and public health workers.

overall neoliberal regime explain serious structural limitations for the labor movement, the growing grassroots movements that are simultaneously emerging, and not only in labor, are to be taken seriously. An unprecedented reemergence of social movements is ripping at the seams of Chile's neoliberal project.

In 2006, with secondary school student protests and Mapuche struggles, we see the first emergence of significant social movements since community and labor struggles against the dictatorship in the 1980s (Schneider 1995; Stillerman 1998). Three important strikes took place in 2007 in new and important sectors of the economy—subcontracted copper workers, forestry workers, and workers in the salmon industry (Aravena and Núñez 2009). The year 2011 brought a renewed student movement with a nine-month student strike that shook the Chilean government and society to its core (see chapter 6). In addition, we also witnessed significant environmental activism and activism on indigenous rights. These grassroots movements provide cautious optimism for the future, despite the fact that the overarching political strategy in Chile is neoliberalism with a human face.

Walmart in Chile

As in many of its international operations, Walmart did not simply open a store in Chile but rather bought out an existing Chilean company in 2009. Generally, international big box stores have not fared well in Chile. JCPenney, Home Depot, and Carrefour all failed in Chile in the 1990s and early 2000s (Calderon 2006). As such, Walmart's strategy of purchasing a majority share in D&S, the third largest and most successful supermarket chain in Chile, was prudent. There are significant parallels in the history of D&S and Walmart that made it the logical choice for acquisition. In order to better understand the relationship, it helps to understand how D&S rose to be a successful player in the retail industry in Chile.

D&S started as a family operated supermarket (Almac) in 1957. It was the first of its kind in Chile and Latin America as a whole (Distribución y Servicios 2014). In 1984, the company introduced a new discount format called Ekono, and by 1987 it opened an Híper Ekono, a large-scale affordable supermarket. By the mid-1990s D&S grew into a small empire, diversifying its operations and adding a construction company (Inmobilaria SAITEC). By 1995, D&S had opened its first Híper Líder (the equivalent of a big box store in the United States). The three final important milestones for D&S were the introduction of the credit card Presto in 1996, the creation of a centralized warehouse (LTS) in 1997, and the acquisition of the French firm Carrefour in 2003. As D&S became more and more successful, it continued to expand. Prior to Walmart's acquisition, it had already created Híper Líder, Líder Express, Ekono, and Acuenta. Walmart has maintained all four of these different formats.

Híper Líder is the closest to what a Super Walmart looks like in the United States. It is both a grocery store and a consumer goods store. While it touts low prices, it is not a discount store, as it targets upper middle class families. Líder Express is a regular sized supermarket, with a few consumer goods. It closely resembles Kroger or Ralphs in the United States, and it targets middle and upper middle class families. Acuenta is the discount warehouse. It is not a wholesale store like Sam's Club, but it is branded as a discount center. As such, it targets working class and lower middle class consumers. Finally, Ekono most closely resembles convenience stores, though slightly larger. It also targets middle and working class consumers. By 2007, D&S controlled 33.5 percent of the retail grocery market with 145 stores (Distribución y Servicios 2014). By 2009, when Walmart acquired a controlling interest in D&S, it had 35 percent of the grocery market.

Walmart and D&S were logical partners, since the latter's owners had long admired the Walmart model. The Walmart model in the United States was initially based, almost exclusively, on free market principles. But soon after opening, Sam Walton recognized the political and geographical importance of the South and incorporated a fundamentalist Christian belief system into his corporate strategy (Moreton 2010). This principle led to the current Walmart model, which draws on hyper individualism and conservative moral values. The Walton's continue to be one of the richest families in the world.

D&S systematically tried to model itself on Walmart (Distribución y Servicios 2014). The Ibáñez family, owners of D&S, are right-wing fundamentalists. They are members of the conservative Catholic organization Opus Dei (González Santibáñez 2011) and actively supported the military coup and Pinochet. They also benefitted from the neoliberal policies that allowed them to expand their enterprise and open a private university named after the family patriarch, Adolfo Ibáñez. The family so admired Pinochet that in D&S's central office in Santiago they had a statue of him that they saluted every morning (Andres, executive committee member, interview 2011).

Neoliberalism, as produced in Chile and then the United States, was the key to the success of both the Ibáñez and Walton families. Without the dictatorship and shock treatment that Chile received in the 1980s D&S would probably have continued to be a rather small retail operation. However, deregulation and shifts in consumer culture allowed it to grow. D&S's growth captured the interest of Walmart, whose global expansion has succeeded while U.S. sales remain stagnant. D&S and Walmart were a natural fit.

Walmart's Model in Chile

Although the parallels between D&S and Walmart are clear, Walmart has nonetheless made changes to its own business model in Chile. These changes have occurred slowly over time. In Walmart's first year, it essentially changed nothing. In its second year, it began to reorganize management and supplier relations, and in the third and fourth year it more aggressively changed corporate culture and negotiated new contracts with unions. Finally, in the fifth year it bought an additional 20 percent share in D&S, leaving the Ibáñez family with only 20 percent share in the company. It also officially changed the corporate name from D&S to Walmart Chile. Walmart has also taken a different approach from D&S in terms of corporate expansion. D&S largely focused on the Híper markets, whereas Walmart has aggressively expanded Ekono and Acuenta stores. In 2014, Walmart controlled over 40 percent of the retail grocery market and had 384 stores (Walmart 2014). These changes to the business model can be categorized in two ways, shifts in types of stores and changing corporate culture.

Shift in Types of Stores

Figure 2.2 represents a side-by-side comparison of the changes that Walmart made in terms of retail stores between 2009 and 2014.

Despite growth in all four types of stores since Walmart's acquisition, the clear strategy has been to develop and expand the small format stores more than the Híper and Líder Express formats. This path is in stark contrast with D&S's strategy of focusing on Híper Líder. In 2011 alone Walmart opened forty-one stores and expanded its credit business to 1.6 million users (Walmart 2014). The main reason Walmart cites for the expansion in Ekono and Acuenta is that the formats "address segments where supermarket penetration is still low and there is room to grow" (Best 2011). In other words, it is expanding in poorer neighborhoods where it is going to have a competitive edge. Expanding to working class and lower middle class neighborhoods also makes sense in terms of the Presto credit card, because these places have only since around 2000 attained access to consumer credit. Walmart happens to be one of the leaders in predatory credit practices in Chile. The Presto credit card has a nearly 40 percent interest rate and no grace period. When people use the credit card, they start accruing interest from the day of purchase, unlike than the U.S. standard of thirty days after purchase. This practice, of course, most penalizes poor and working class people who do not earn enough to pay off the balance of the credit card immediately. Furthermore, many poorer consumers are purchasing basic food necessities such as milk, bread, and eggs at Walmart, because they do not have the money to pay for these items in cash at the small businesses in their communities. Thus, they pay a double penalty: higher prices for these basic necessities at Walmart and interest on top of that. It may seem contradictory that basic necessities cost more at Walmart, so it bears repeating that Walmart in Chile, with the exception of Ekono stores, is mostly targeted at a middle and upper middle class consumer. However, with increasing access to credit, working class consumers are shopping more at Ekono and Líder markets. Walmart relies on these cash-strapped consumers to make purchases on credit. In many cases it is cheaper to purchase eggs, milk, and bread from the small local corner store, but these stores often accept only cash, driving many of their traditional consumers to large grocers.

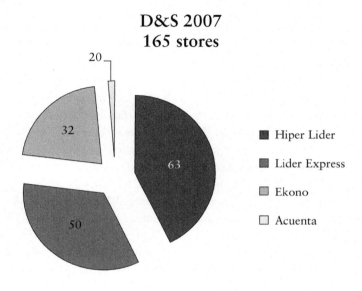

D&S 2007
165 stores

- ■ Hiper Lider
- ■ Lider Express
- ■ Ekono
- □ Acuenta

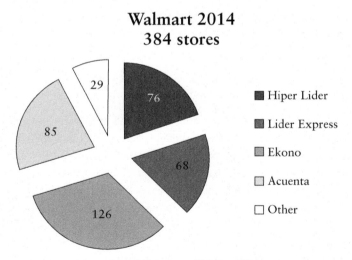

Walmart 2014
384 stores

- ■ Hiper Lider
- ■ Lider Express
- ■ Ekono
- □ Acuenta
- □ Other

Figure 2.2. Shift in stores D&S vs. Walmart
Source: Data from Walmart and D&S websites

Changing Corporate Culture

In its second and third years of operation in Chile, Walmart made a number of significant changes. First, it changed its tax ID from D&S to Walmart Chile. Second, even though it has not changed the names of the stores to Walmart, it has begun an advertising campaign that makes clear that Líder, Ekono, and Acuenta are all part of Walmart. The ads essentially tell the consumer that Líder can offer rock-bottom prices because it is part of and supported by the world's largest corporation. Finally, it began more systematically implementing its corporate culture, especially in retail stores. Workers noted a dramatic shift in shopfloor practices towards the end of 2010 and the beginning of 2011. Store managers started handing out new employee handbooks with the Walmart logo. It officially started calling workers *colaboradores* (similar to the U.S. "associates"), and it also began requiring that workers look a certain way. For example, women who regularly wear nail polish were asked to wear light colored nail polish (Andrea, worker, interview 2011). Walmart also began to implement its trademark chanting and instituted programs such as employee of the month. Most important, Walmart has tried to implement its "open door" policy as a way to get employees to individually negotiate with managers instead of going through their union. These changes in corporate culture have led to increasing worker grievances.

Conclusion

The neoliberal experiments in Chile and the United States have had significant, serious, long-term consequences for workers and their families. Elites in both countries imposed extreme deregulation and privatization. Workers in both countries have experienced eroding wages and working conditions while seeing sharp increases in consumer debt. The neoliberal model has contributed and facilitated the growth of big business and especially big box chain stores. In order to survive, grow, and prosper Walmart has had to redesign itself for urban and global markets. The company's net sales reveal the impact of its global operations. In the 2015 fiscal year, U.S. net sales were approximately $346 billion. In its global operations, net sales were approximately $136 billion. About 28 percent of Walmart's net sales came from its global operations (Walmart 2015). Chile has become an important contributor to Walmart's global strategy, but as in other global locations, Walmart has not been able to impose its model wholesale. It has had to evaluate and make sense of the Chilean institutional context and culture and adapt its practices accordingly. Herein lies the tension between Walmart and its workers and where the opportunity to challenge this behemoth begins.

3

LEVERAGING POWER

Two Models of Successful Unionism

> Como el conocido relato biblico, el enemigo un verdadero Goliat,
> con formación militar, lleno de armaduras, escudo, lanza y jabalina,
> nosotros como David, solamente con la fe del deber tener que luchar,
> sin armas, sin preparación, sin estrategia militar. Entonces ¿Cómo
> pudimos vencer?, simplemente porque "no teniamos miedo." Lo
> enfrentamos con todo y el enemigo fue doblegado.
>
> Just like the well-known biblical tale; the enemy a true Goliath with
> military training, armor, shield, and spears. We were like David, only
> with the faith of knowing we had to struggle, without arms, without
> preparation, without military strategy. So, how were we able to win?
> Simply because "we were not afraid." We confronted him with all we
> had and the enemy gave in.
>
> —VILLAGRA SOTO (2010; AUTHOR TRANSLATION)

The biblical tale of David and Goliath is a powerful one that in many ways represents the struggle of Chilean workers against Walmart and its predecessor D&S. Rodrigo, president of the warehouse workers union since 2010, points to that story when I interviewed him in 2011 to describe the union's struggle for justice in the workplace. He argues that courage helped them win against the world's largest transnational organization. Though it is true that courage played a role in the battle, in this chapter I argue that Walmart warehouse and retail workers have made significant gains because they succeeded in understanding their target and were able to mobilize different sets of resources. How do we make sense of these workers' power in light of declining union density, a weak traditional labor movement, and the increasing flexibilization of labor? Like David, they understood that they had nothing close to the financial and political resources of D&S and then Walmart. Like David, they understood that they would have to outsmart their enemy, rather than overpower it. Workers, both in retail and warehouse, created innovative, militant, strategic, and democratic unions that have served them well over the years.

Each of the Chilean Walmart unions that I have been working with mobilizes its resources (autonomy, strategy, militancy, democratic participation) in a unique way, based on its own context, industry, and particular union culture of its sector. How a union mobilizes its resources affects its outcomes (for more on this, see chapters 4 and 5). So while both the warehouse and retail unions have been successful, they have achieved success in diverse ways and through different models. I call these models "strategic democracy" (warehouse) and "flexible militancy" (retail). The retail and warehouse workers' capacity for disruption, their basis of social power, is shaped by structural and associational powers (see chapter 1). Structural power is based on workers' structural location in an industry, while associational power is based on the collective organization of workers (Wright 2000). As we will see, the warehouse union, because of its location in the logistics industry, has both structural and associational power. The retail unions, by contrast, have little structural power, but a relatively high level of associational power. One significant similarity is that both of these groups are autonomous from the mainstream labor movement and the Chilean political structure.[1] None of the independent federations and unions are affiliated with Chile's largest labor federation, the Central Unitaria de Trabajadores (CUT), and only one of the independent retail federations, Federación Nacional de Trabajadores Líder (FENATRALID), is affiliated with the Commercial Workers Labor Federation. Although individual workers may be connected with political parties and tendencies,

---

1. Historically it has been common for some Chilean unions, for example coal miners, to be directly affiliated with a political party (e.g., Socialist Party, Communist Party). Even when union leaderships were contested, their leaders had clear party affiliations and political aspirations within their parties. The independent Walmart unions are unaffiliated, and their leaders are not particularly involved in party politics. This position gives them the space to not be influenced by political parties.

TABLE 3.1. Distribution of characteristics among warehouse and retail unions

		LTS	FENATRALID	Federación Autónoma	Ekono
	Associational power	×	×	×	×
	Structural power	×			
Union democracy	Membership Participation/ decision making	×	×	×	
	Formal democracy	×	×	×	×
	Leadership development	×		×	
Strategic capacity	Highly motivated	×	×	×	×
	Salient knowledge	×	×	×	
	Learning from deliberation	×	×	×	
Militancy	Direct action		×	×	×
	Strikes	×	×		×

they generally do not have party aspirations, and these unions as a whole do not participate in political parties.

To recap, militancy, strategic capacity, and union democracy are all important variables that help explain how Walmart workers in Chile have built strong associational power, thereby improving their capacity for disruption, and ultimately forcing Walmart to meet many worker demands. In addition, warehouse workers have the structural power to disrupt production. Because Walmart retail and warehouse workers have access to different kinds of resources, they have developed two successful union models—*strategic democracy* and *flexible militancy*. These can be explained by industry differences, the way in which the union was organized, and political histories. Table 3.1 shows the distribution of all of these different characteristics among the warehouse and retail unions. Important differences in industry partly explain the variances in the histories of the warehouse versus retail unions.

Logistics Sector

Growth in the logistics sector since 2000 is closely connected with Chile's shift from the import-substitution model in place before the dictatorship, to the export-oriented model that has been in place since the dictatorship. However, radical advancements in technology and the signing of free trade agreements in the Concertación era have also significantly changed the industry. As a result, the logistics industry has been growing at a steady rate of 10 to 15 percent per year (Negocios Globales 2016). For example, in 2009 there were already over 750,000 square meters (approximately 200 acres) of warehousing space concentrated in four areas on the outskirts of Santiago (Cintron 2009). The industry has recognized that large, centralized warehouses are more efficient and productive than individual warehouses attached to stores. Large supermarkets have been innovators in this respect. As recently as 2000 many large supermarkets in Chile had warehouses directly attached to them, with goods transported from port to store. However, the rapidly increasing retail sector made this system incredibly inefficient and expensive. As of 2016, a majority of supermarkets have moved to a centralized distribution system that goes from port to centralized warehouse to retail stores. Sometimes these centralized warehouses service several different companies, but Walmart Chile owns and operates its own warehouses.

Growth in the logistics sector has produced opportunities and challenges for workers. On the one hand, the industry has benefitted from changes in the labor code that have given management increasing flexibility, especially in part-time employment and subcontracted work (Echeverría 2010). As of 2015, workers in the industry earned an average of U.S. $573 per month, compared to U.S. $350, the minimum wage in Chile (Durán and Kremerman 2015). This wage has not allowed them to meet their basic necessities. Their work is physically challenging, and they often labor under bad working conditions in warehouses that are either too hot or too cold. These workers also tend to be invisible in the supply chain, often working in spatially segregated zones on the outskirts of Santiago. On the other hand, the concentration of warehousing into a centralized distribution system has created the conditions for structural power. Logistics is a key part of the supply chain, and disruptions such as protests, slow-downs, and strikes in the warehouse industry can paralyze the entire supply chain (Bonacich and Wilson 2008; Silver 2003). However, we have not seen widespread organizing in the warehouse sector of the logistics industry in Chile to date.

In contrast to the general state of the logistics sector, which is plagued by low wages, bad working conditions, and subcontracted labor, Walmart logistics workers have some of the highest wages in the industry, better working conditions, and limited subcontracted labor. For example, in 2015 the LTS union wages averaged U.S. $800 a month, compared to the U.S. $573 average for the industry. How can we explain this dramatic contrast? In short, it's not enough to have industry leverage or structural power. Workers must also have associational power. As a class, logistics workers have a significant amount of disruptive power (Bonacich and Wilson 2008; Silver 2003), but if they are not organized or don't know how to leverage their power, this structural power has little value. In general there is a lot of variation in how logistics workers leverage their power in Chile. For example, port workers are able to leverage their power very strategically and are also organized and earn high wages. But this phenomenon is relatively recent, as port workers have long been excluded from labor law, because of their economic importance. As such, they have had to organize outside of legal frameworks. Truck drivers, also part of the logistics industry are more complicated to make sense of. They have structural power, but they operate as independent contractors, so the sense of collective identity and class-consciousness is complicated. Warehouse workers are also a mixed bag. Many do not know how to leverage their power. However, Walmart warehouse workers are an example of a group that has figured out the power of organization, democracy, strategy, and leverage.

Walmart logistics workers in Chile have benefitted from a centralized distribution system in which the three main Walmart warehouses for the entire country are located in Santiago. Therefore a strike would paralyze the supply chain. Organizing a union (and in particular the kind of union they created) gave them the capacity to use their structural power effectively and make steady improvements to their wages and working conditions. As Silver (2003, 96) astutely observes, "the greater capital's vulnerability to workers' direct action and the more limited the options for pursuing a spatial fix solution, the more employers would feel compelled to accommodate workers' demands and grievances." In other words, Walmart warehouse workers have figured out how to leverage their power, while at the same time Walmart has limited access to a "spatial fix," or the ability to move the warehouses to another location where workers are unorganized. They did open a non-union warehouse, which was unionized within a couple of years. The retail industry, however, has had a different development.

Retail Sector

Since the mid-1990s the Chilean retail sector has exploded. In 2014 the retail sector represented 22 percent of Chile's gross domestic product, up from 8 percent in the 1990s (Durán and Kremerman 2015). As of 2008, the sector employed over 1.2 million Chileans and represented nearly 20 percent of overall employment in the country. Originally the sector employed nearly equal numbers of men and women (Durán and Kremerman 2008), but over time it has become increasingly feminized. There are a number of reasons for the rapid rise of the retail sector. First, the implementation of the neoliberal regime greatly expanded consumption (see chapter 2). Second, retail power has been concentrated in the hands of a few corporations (Cencosud, Falabella, D&S, and Ripley), which have been very strategic in both their national and international development. Many have bought out small national chains, developed a financial services component (credit cards, which yield 7 to 10 percent of total revenue), and expanded to neighboring countries such as Peru, Argentina, and Brazil, when the national market neared saturation in the 1990s (Calderon 2006). In fact, the financial services division in retail has not only proven to be profitable to the industry but has also been responsible for sparking consumer credit access and consumption in the entire country. Ossandón (2014) argues that the supermarket industry and department stores pursue a strategy known as "sowing" in order to attract new clients. This strategy offers people of low socioeconomic status, who might not have access to credit through a bank, the opportunity to obtain store credit. To minimize risk, retailers offer small amounts of credit, usually less than US$100. Although some people won't pay back this small loan, many more will, and that is a good way to hook people on credit. If people are responsible with their payments, their credit line gradually increases. Of those with credit debt, nearly 50 percent owe their debt to retailers, whereas only 26 percent owe their debt to banks (Ossandón 2014). It is easy to see why retailers have spent significant energies expanding their financial services divisions.

In addition to financial services, really a side operation, the retail sector in Chile has mostly concentrated its energies in department stores, supermarkets, and home improvement stores. In the early 2000s Chile began experimenting with "integrated retailing" after industry analysts came to the realization that they could not achieve sufficient scale in their limited domestic market. At that point firms started consolidating. For example, the department store Falabella bought out some home improvement stores and later the supermarket Tottus. Cencosud, another retail giant, owned Jumbo, a large supermarket chain, and bought Almacenes Paris, a department store (Calderon 2006). These kinds of massive conglomerations have been very successful. Finally, changes in the organization of work have dramatically changed the retail industry. In particular, the flexibilization of labor and the growth and expansion of part-time and temporary work, night and weekend shifts, subcontracting, and poly-functionality[2] have all been contributing factors to the refashioning of the industry (Palacios-Valladares 2011; Stecher et al. 2010). As recently as the early 1990s, department stores and even supermarkets in Chile had shorter Saturday hours and were closed on Sunday. New forms of work organization have made it cost effective and in fact very profitable for the retail industry in Chile to sustain longer store hours and open on Sundays.

Figure 3.1, produced by the nonprofit Fundación Sol in Chile, shows the rapid increase in market share by supermarket chains from 1996 to 2006. We see the strong growth of D&S and Jumbo, while the "Other" category diminishes significantly in terms of market share by 2006. Between 2006 and 2010, market share stabilizes, particularly that of the merged conglomerates Cencosud/Jumbo and D&S/Walmart. During this period Cencosud Jumbo holds about 30 percent market share while D&S holds about 33 percent.

Demographics of Workers in the Retail Industry

Workers in the Chilean retail industry tend to be young, have low levels of education (many haven't completed high school), and have low socioeconomic status (Stecher et al. 2010). The average industry wage in 2010 was about 247,000 pesos or US$465 a month. This amount is nearly 30 percent above the minimum wage in Chile, which at the time was 193,000 pesos or US$363 per month. Over 50 percent of women in the labor market work in the retail industry and 60 percent of young people under age

2. *Polyfuncionalidad* or polyfunctional workers in English refers to different workplace tasks performed by the same worker, for example, a baker who also stocks shelves.

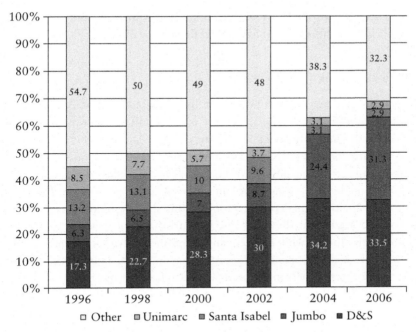

Figure 3.1. Supermarket chains' increase in market share, 1996

Source: Gonzalo Durán, Fundación Sol, based on ASACH and FNE Data. Translated by author.

thirty-five are employed in it. Yet retail also employs a significant number of workers over forty-five. Stecher (2012) reports that the industry essentially hires people with few or no options for other employment. As in the United States, retail workers did not always fit this profile. Until the early 1990s the retail industry was very similar to the one Lichtenstein (2010) describes in the United States. Traditional retail workers in Chile were middle-class people who earned decent wages and were able to provide excellent customer service. They felt a sense of professionalism and were loyal to their firm. A majority of them worked in large department stores that were unionized (Stecher 2012). By contrast, the model since the 1990s has completely changed, and the project of hiring young, working-class people has served the industry well. Retail is the ultimate precarious employer, and the industry has deeply profited from its transformation. Retail workers are no longer particularly loyal to their employer, nor do they receive extensive training (Stecher 2012). They understand that they are considered cheap and disposable labor, and as a result they largely see their jobs as short-term obligations rather than careers.

Rise of Unions in the Retail Sector

Unionization has increased dramatically in the retail sector. According to Fundación Sol, in 2011, 22 percent of the retail sector was unionized, compared with only about 12 percent in 2000 (Durán 2011). This figure is in stark contrast to the United States where in 2011 only 5.4 percent of the retail sector was unionized. Limited academic research has been conducted on this interesting rise of unionization in the retail sector. There are a few potential explanatory factors for this spike in union density. First, I would argue that the labor law reforms that took place in the 1990s and early 2000s, while modest and often ineffective, potentially served to create a slight opening for organizing in Chile. Labor law reforms gave workers some protection against arbitrary firing, made employers legally responsible for protecting the rights of subcontracted workers, reduced the workweek from forty-eight to forty-five hours, limited overtime, guaranteed nondiscrimination, and established unemployment insurance (Palacios-Valladares 2011). These reforms benefitted all workers, but they especially benefitted female workers, who are more likely to be subcontracted and arbitrarily dismissed and discriminated against, especially during childbearing years. It is possible that these minimal protections helped foster an environment for organizing, especially of women who have recently flooded the retail sector.

A second important factor in the rise of union density may be related to women's labor force participation. Research indicates that, globally, women workers are more likely to unionize than men (Yates 2006). At the very least they are more sympathetic to the idea of unions. Female participation in the Chilean labor market has dramatically increased in the last decade. In 1990, female labor force participation was 32 percent; by 2014, it had jumped to 49 percent (World Bank 2016). At the same time, we see impressive increases in women's unionization rates. In 2002, union density among women was 8.2 percent; by 2013, it was 12.7 percent. Furthermore, the increase among women is double that of men for the same period (Riquelme y Abarca 2015). Although it is to be expected that women's increased labor force participation would yield increased levels of unionization, it is surprising that women's unionization rates have increased faster than their labor force participation (Riquelme y Abarca 2015). Women tend to be concentrated in the service sector, including commerce (and within that retail), communications, education, medical services, banking and insurance services, and personal services. In Chile, as in the United States, the labor code is weaker in terms of agricultural and domestic workers. Therefore retail is one of the most important low-wage industries where the law protects the right to organize. Thus the influx of women into the retail industry most likely has had some effect on unionization rates.

Finally and most important, the conglomeration of the retail industry in Chile has benefitted not only retailers, by allowing them to expand and change the conditions of work, but in some sense it has also benefitted workers by concentrating them in big box stores, thereby making it easier to organize. Again, Riquelme and Albarca's (2015) study is instructive, pointing out that unions are mostly concentrated in large firms. According to the Encuesta Laboral (Encla) 2011 survey, 48 percent of large companies (1,000 or more workers) are unionized, whereas only 23 percent of medium firms and 4.5 percent of small firms have unions. Furthermore, nearly 80 percent of unionized women work in large firms. This makes sense since it is easier to unionize one firm with 1,000 employees than it is to organize 100 firms with only ten employees each. Another way of thinking about it is that a concentration of workers in one place has the potential to foster associational power. From a historical perspective, we can think of the unionization of large auto plants and steel mills. Retail has traditionally been harder to organize because there has not been a high concentration of the workforce in any one store. Big box stores have changed this dynamic. In Chile, stores like Híper Líder, Jumbo, Tottus, Easy, and Home Center that measure between 80,000 and 100,000 square feet have concentrated workforces. On average, these big stores employ 350 to 400 workers. This figure is significantly different from small retail stores, which are numerous but employ only five or ten people. I would argue that the concentration of the retail workforce in large firms has facilitated unionization and therefore contributed to an increase in union density in the retail sector.

In short, a combination of modest labor law reforms that have particularly benefitted women, women's concentration in retail, and the concentration of workers in big box stores (increasingly feminized) gives us at least a partial understanding of why there is higher union density in the retail sector than the national average.

The History of Walmart Unions in Chile

As sectoral differences create different kinds of structural, associational, and symbolic power, so Walmart's unions in Chile have varied histories. Table 3.2 shows the tremendous variation in the different independent Walmart unions. Warehouse workers are often invisible, behind-the-scenes workers, but they have the potential to disrupt and paralyze an entire supply chain. They also have the advantage of workplace density or concentration so that one union represents thousands of workers. Retail workers, by contrast, are visible as the public face of the company. Therefore, they have the tools to potentially wage a more public battle against their employer, or symbolic leverage. However, because there are hundreds of Walmart stores across the length of the country it is harder for retail workers to wage effective strikes. Furthermore, because Walmart retail workers are represented by over eighty different unions, it is difficult to have the kind of industry leverage that the warehouse workers have with only one union. Walmart has so many unions because unions can only operate at the enterprise level, unless a company agrees to negotiate across unions (see chapter 2). Also, until 2014, Chilean employers were able to use multiple tax identification numbers to represent different parts of one company (called multirut). Perhaps this was not the intention of the law, but it served as an effective union-busting tactic, because enterprise unions formed under a single company's distinct tax identification numbers, and the law barred a company from negotiating across its different tax identification numbers. Walmart had many different tax identification numbers until the 2014 multirut law forced it to narrow down its number to four different entities. Thus in 2016, Walmart had tax identification numbers for Supermarkets (four formats), Líder Servicios Financieros (financial services division), Walmart Logistics, and Walmart Chile Inmobilaria (real estate). Nonetheless, these changes have been recent and the history of how the unions were established dates to 2006, so while the

TABLE 3.2. Variation among Walmart unions in 2012

	LTS/warehouse union	Federación Autónoma/ retail federation-	FENATRALID/retail federation	Ekono union/retail union
Year founded	2006	2010	2007	2011
Gender of members	90 percent men	80 percent women	80 percent women	60 percent women
No. of members	2,000	2,500	1,500	800
Workplace concentration	Members in two main warehouses (1,200 in one and 800 in the other)	Members dispersed across Hiper (350–400 per store), Express (150–200 per store), and Ekono (10 per store)	Members dispersed across Hiper (350–400 per store) and Express (150–200 per store)	Members only at Ekono across all of Chile (10 per store)
Strategic power	High because it controls distribution of goods	Low because small membership means less disruptive capacity	Low because small membership means less disruptive capacity	Lowest because membership is small and dispersed
Leadership background	Strongest union/ social movement experience	New to unions but has mixed social movement organizing experience	New to unions. Very little other organizing experience	Mixed union and social movement experience
Affiliation with national and international labor organizations	Unaffiliated	Unaffiliated	Unaffiliated (previously affiliated with Union Network International (UNI- Global)	Unaffiliated

multirut law has affected the number of entities that Walmart has in Chile, it has not yet affected the organization of its labor unions.

Warehouse Workers: LTS Union

In 2006, when D&S still owned Líder and the warehouse Logística, Transportación y Servicios (LTS), a group of workers started meeting to talk about unionizing. They were tired of the low wages and the lack of dignity and respect on the job. In 2006, the average wage for an LTS warehouse worker was only US$350 per month. Workers felt they had no voice: They couldn't complain, or make suggestions. Workers who did stand up for themselves were often ignored or worse, retaliated against (Jorge, executive committee member). Furthermore, because the workers didn't know how wages and productivity bonuses were calculated, they were cheated out of part of their salaries on a regular basis (Sindicato de Trabajadores Bodegas LTS 2010). In addition, workers were forced to work ten to twenty hour shifts when products came in, and they were always nervous about getting fired (Sindicato de Trabajadores Bodegas LTS 2010).

Cristián, the union's part-time lawyer, says, "We started the union slowly and covertly. At first it was only twenty of us workers, then we kept talking to people and getting them to join us" (interview 2011). After several months of covert organizing, the group had enough signatures to declare themselves an official union on May 24, 2006. Although many of the workers did not have experience with unions, some did, and their experiences were generally not very positive. The executive committee members of the newly founded union all committed to building "a real union." For these workers this meant on the ground participation and leadership by the rank-and-file. As union president Rodrigo says,

> If you involve people, if you create a project with them, people feel motivated. When decisions are made collectively, the responsibility for those decisions belongs to the collective, and not only to the union leadership. This is what is different. A bad collective decision is a bad decision by all [workers], which is different from a bad decision made by the union leadership, which is only the decision of a few. (Villagra 2010, 28; author translation).

The union leadership and rank-and-file were first careful to create a union structure that would maximize participation and democratic decision making. This task was not easy. Some union members simply wanted the union to make all the decisions and fight all the battles without themselves having to commit. However, the union leadership understood that without a grassroots movement behind them they would eventually lose the war. Once again, Rodrigo points out,

> I think that the union reflects all of the contradictions that we hold. We look for the collective, while many times people look for the individual. All people work for money and work for their families, so getting workers to think collectively is really hard, especially since we live in this individualistic system which is one hundred percent backed up by television, radio, and the media in general. It is a constant struggle for union leaders to say that the collective is what's important, not the individual. (Villagra 2010, 29; author translation)

The union leadership and many of the rank-and-file members take pride in prioritizing the collective. Serious one-on-one organizing, careful conversations, and trust building slowly convinced workers that negotiating as a collective had greater potential to yield results than negotiating individually with the company. Given D&S's hostility toward the union, building a union that worked collectively was especially important, because the leadership knew that they would have to go on strike to obtain their first contract. Ultimately, workers voted unanimously to go on strike in November 2006.

In the end, the union was able to negotiate a first contract that included a few gains: an end-of-strike bonus, transportation benefit, a no-interest loan for workers, and a bulletin board for posting union announcements (2006 collective bargaining agreement). Despite the modesty of these gains, the strike had a significant effect in building a movement. Though union leaders were not able to make all the gains they had hoped for in the first contract, they did gain legitimacy and credibility, whereas the company lost credibility. Workers experienced collective decision making and felt that the union had represented their issues at the table, even if they were not able to win everything they thought they deserved. Management, by contrast, had tried to coopt workers and offered them benefits that they weren't able to deliver. Carlos, a worker, states "managers told us we would get extra raises if we didn't join the union, but when the contract was settled they said there were no extra funds, so many of us who were suspicious of the union ended up joining it later" (interview 2011). The strike changed workers who had never experienced participating in a labor action. Cristián says, "after the strike workers held their heads high, they demanded respect, and displayed confidence I had never seen before" (interview 2011). Strikers had learned an invaluable lesson in what it means to fight the boss, and they became very engaged in the day-to-day activities of running the union. They were invested in their union and wanted to show other workers what it truly meant to have a democratic, bottom-up union. Federico, a worker, states, "I was excited to become a representative [of my area] and have the opportunity to talk to colleagues about our union" (interview 2011). Even nonstrikers saw firsthand what it meant to take risks, go on strike, and win dignity. LTS's strike was instrumental in setting up the groundwork for creating a different kind of union.

LTS Leadership Politics

The political experience and diversity of LTS leaders also profoundly shaped the union's trajectory. Their range of experience has facilitated the union's strategic capacity and fostered a dynamic process of decision making. Some of the older workers have a history of union participation or participation in movements against the dictatorship. Some founding members of the union are socialists or leftists of some kind. Rodrigo, the president since 2010 interestingly does not have a labor background but was raised in the evangelical church and sees his union activism as a calling. Jorge, a member of the executive committee, had to take care of his three siblings when his parents were forced underground in 1978, one of the most brutal years of the dictatorship. He was only twelve years old and had to rely on neighbors for food. Most of the younger members of the union do not have political histories, but they receive considerable political education in the union. For example, in order to join the union soccer team members have to attend the *escuela sindical* (union school) once a week. One of the most important characteristics that distinguishes the warehouse union from the independent retail unions is the warehouse union's unwavering commitment to political education. In addition to the executive committee the union employs a part-time lawyer, Cristián, and a former exile, Ivan, participates in the daily life of the union as a volunteer, particularly on issues of political education. Both Cristián and Ivan have played a formative role in LTS. Cristián has helped the organization leverage labor law to their advantage and has been instrumental in advising the union during collective bargaining negotiations. He also trains LTS members on Chilean labor law and workplace rights. Furthermore, he comes from a union family and is himself committed to bottom-up organizing and democratic unionism. Ivan comes from the older generation of trade union leaders, was an activist during the Allende years, and has a wealth of experience with popular education. After the coup he was exiled to Germany.

The combination of industrial leverage, democratic union building, and a certain brand of leadership politics has allowed LTS to operate from a position of strength vis-à-vis Walmart (see chapter 4). Because the union had solid roots when Walmart bought D&S, it has been able to be proactive in its relationship with Walmart, frequently anticipating company moves and being on the frontlines of strategic decision making. As such they have been able to leverage their strong associational and structural power to effectively threaten the disruption of production in order to achieve their victories. The history of the independent retail unions is very different.

History of Walmart Retail Unions

There are about 38,000 Walmart retail workers in Chile. These workers are spread across the four format stores (Híper Líder, Líder Express, Ekono, and Acuenta) and are represented by over eighty enterprise level unions and five federations. Only 5,000 of these workers are represented by militant, democratic, autonomous unions. These unions, in turn, are members of two retail federations (Federación Autónoma and FENATRALID), which represent the seventeen unions that I worked with during my time in Chile.[3] The other workers are either not unionized (about 16,000), represented by the company union (about 14,000), or are members of one of three other Walmart retail worker federations (about 3,000). Two of these other federations were created after my 2011 fieldwork. I did not have access to the other older federation. Much like the Federación Autónoma and FENATRALID the newest federations are autonomous organizations. None of them has pursued democratic unionism as a model. However, one of the federations is quite militant and launched a significant if unsuccessful strike in December 2014.

The Federación Autónoma and FENATRALID and their unions are motivated by deep disdain for the leader of the company union and the deals he struck with Walmart. Many of the founders of the autonomous unions were previously active union members in the company union. Seeing firsthand the negotiations between the company union and Walmart made them realize that they needed to break away from that union and form unions of their own. For example, Sandra, president of Federación Autónoma, shared in an interview that when she was an activist in the company union she saw firsthand a copy of a payment (sent by fax) from Walmart to the president of the company union. The president of the company union had apparently been receiving US$2,000 per month to maintain labor peace. Given that many workers in Chile make $350 to $400 per month, it is a sizeable amount on top of his salary.

In order to better understand the split between the company union and the autonomous unions, it may help to know how the company union came to exist. In 2007, the Walmart intra-enterprise union Sindicato interempresa Líder (SIL) was formed and soon after that started negotiating with D&S (González Santibáñez 2011; Cristián, lawyer, interview 2011). The leader of the SIL had been a union leader at the French chain Carrefour, and when D&S bought some of the Carrefour locations, he struck a deal with D&S. The agreement was basically one of labor-management cooperation. This approach is consistent with various service sector unions in Palacios Valladares (2011) earlier study of unionism in Chile. As Juan, the president of the SIL, explains it, "D&S was very antiunion, and in order to get my foot in the door, I told them that if they accepted

---

3. Each union has its own history and development, but I won't elaborate on these seventeen distinct histories.

me, I wouldn't make trouble. Some people call me a sellout for this, but it's thanks to me that we even have a union" (interview 2011). D&S did not fight the SIL, betting that this union would probably benefit them by keeping the troublemakers out. The SIL grew quickly, and in 2008 it negotiated its first agreement with D&S (Juan, president of the SIL, interview 2011). The agreement was a *convenio colectivo* (agreement/ code-of-conduct), not a collective bargaining agreement. The biggest difference between these two kinds of negotiations is that workers do not have the right to strike under a convenio colectivo. Furthermore, whereas union leaders who negotiate a collective bargaining agreement have immunity against dismissal for union activities, those who negotiate the *convenios colectivos* have neither immunity nor the right to strike (Gariazzo 2007). Convenios colectivos are akin to what are called "sweetheart contracts" in the United States. They provide benefits for the employer in terms of labor peace, with few actual benefits for workers (Gariazzo 2007; González Santibáñez and Consejo de Trabajadores Walmart Chile 2011). The agreement between the SIL and D&S, known as the Acuerdo Marco, set the bar very low on wages while creating high expectations for worker productivity. Included in the Acuerdo Marco were a two percent wage increase, transportation benefit, small bonuses for Christmas and Chilean Independence Day, a uniform, attendance and punctuality bonus, an individual productivity bonus, and a bonus for "constructive" union activities (Acuerdo Marco 2008). Although these benefits somewhat improved the lives of workers who previously had no benefits, the Acuerdo had several serious drawbacks. First, and perhaps most important, the Acuerdo established a precedent that no union could negotiate a collective bargaining agreement with better benefits than those negotiated in the Acuerdo. In other words it created a cap, limiting the ability for unions to negotiate better contracts, thus ensuring low labor costs for Walmart. Second, the agreement created unreasonable demands on workers. For example, in order to actually obtain the attendance and punctuality bonus, workers could not miss a single day of work in the month. If a worker was verifiably sick with a medical certificate and missed a day of work, she would no longer be eligible for the bonus. Therefore very few workers were able to obtain the bonus, which was critical for them because wages were so low. Finally, the bonus for "constructive" union activity was given only to workers who specifically agreed to join the SIL union and who agreed with the union's position on labor peace and labor management coop-eration. This requirement was later ruled illegal and an antiunion prac-tice (Acuerdo Marco 2008; Sindicato Empresa Líder Express-Plaza Italia 2008). In essence this agreement set a damaging precedent for the future of collective bargaining at D&S. As González Santibáñez and Consejo de Trabajadores Walmart Chile (2011) write in a report that was used to testify against Walmart in the South African tribunals,[4]

> The signing of the sweetheart agreement guaranteed the company that there wouldn't be any individual stores in the chain that enter contract negoti-ations that end in conflict. It also established a schedule of contracts that given Chilean labor law, assured that workers would not be able to coordi-nate their individual contract negotiations. The old adage, "divide and rule" was applied rigorously.
>
> The aggregate effect of this process was to achieve labor control and manage the growing wave of conflicts that the company faced. This gave D&S the ability to negotiate its sale to Walmart as a company that was per-ceived as having labor peace.

In 2009, the Chilean courts ruled against D&S for having colluded with the SIL and engaged in antiunion practices. The SIL was also disciplined for constituting a union monopoly and obstructing freedom to choose a union (Court of Appeals San Miguel 2011; González Santibáñez 2012). In 2010, the SIL signed its second agreement, now with Walmart proper. This agreement essentially reproduced the same conditions as the first agreement and was denounced as a protection contract by many of the autonomous unions that had split from the SIL in 2009.

Given the cozy relationship between management and the SIL, work-ers began to join the various autonomous unions. They started out very small but have since grown significantly. The largest federation, Feder-ación Autónoma, now has well over 2,000 members. This growth is in

---

4. Walmart began the process of entering South Africa in 2010, and after the South Af-rican competition hearings and tribunals that took place in 2011, Walmart acquired ma-jority stake in South Africa's Massmart. Walmart used Chile as its model labor relations system to address the South African labor movement's concerns about bad labor practices. The Chilean unions wrote a report used by the South African labor movement documenting its anti-unionism.

contrast to the majority of cases in Palacios-Valladares's 2011 study of collective bargaining dynamics in fifty-three firms in democratic Chile. In the industries she studied, including commerce, militant unions tended to lose membership to the more bureaucratic union that used the strategy of labor-management partnership. Ironically, the Pinochet labor code that has been so detrimental to worker power in Chile as a whole, in this instance, has opened some space for these independent unions to form alongside the company union, since the labor code allows multiple unions to exist in one workplace. It remains to be seen if these smaller unions can effectively (and massively) organize workers away from the SIL. To be sure they have been building power by showing that strategy, militancy, and union democracy are relevant for challenging even the largest trans-national corporation. They have also demonstrated that achieving union density, while important, is not the most significant aspect of labor orga-nizing. Sandra, president of the autonomous union, has stated numerous times that she prefers to take a slow approach to building her union and federation: "I want to do it right. I want workers to understand what they are getting into and what is expected of them as union members. It is not worth building a large organization if workers don't have a clear under-standing of what we are fighting for" (interview 2012).

Although the autonomous retail unions represent the fewest workers, of the 38,000 at Walmart Chile, they have achieved the greatest capacity to break with the pattern agreement and win real wage and benefit in-creases across the board, gains that have spilled over even to the company union. Furthermore, these small independent unions have also been at the forefront of noneconomic victories, particularly with regard to Walmart culture (chapter 5).

Leadership Politics of Retail Unions

Unlike the leaders of the warehouse unions, the leaders of the indepen-dent retail unions do not have significant generational diversity or ex-perience in politics. Based on my interviews it was clear that most of these worker leaders have had little or no experience with unions, as they tend to be women who have come out of domestic, agricultural, or other nonunion retail jobs. Some of these workers have had experi-ences in community-based social movements, and some were also active in antidictatorship organizing, but the vast majority are new to organizing in general. Of the retail union activists I interviewed only about 10 percent had some kind of direct social movement experience, compared to nearly 25 percent of the LTS union activists. However, union leaders at Walmart retail have a number of important things in common. They believe that the mainstream Chilean labor movement has relied too much on electoral politics, especially on the Concertación, for labor gains. They believe that the workers' movement must be independent from electoral politics, particularly political parties, and that it must be generated from the bottom up. Perhaps most important, they believe that the SIL has a deleterious effect on building worker power at Walmart. They have come to these realizations based on their experiences as workers and seeing the difficulties in achieving a fair labor law reform, their reading of labor history, and their experiences in the SIL union. These points of commonality have created a sense of solidarity between some of the different independent unions and federations and have allowed them to work together on key issues in contract negotiations.

Given these politics, these leaders believe that they must remain independent from the mainstream labor federation, the CUT, and politicians. Each of these unions has its own strengths and weaknesses. Some are better at developing leaders and base building; these tend to have presidents or executive-committee members with some level of political experience, like some of the leaders in the FENATRALID. Others have good formal democratic procedures but are struggling on the path. The Ekono union, for example, started out gravitating towards building a grassroots democratic union. For a couple of years after the strike they created formal democratic procedures and developed a strategy for membership involvement across a multitude of stores, but in 2014 the leadership joined the SIL union. According to Esteban, a former leader of the Ekono union, running the union was hard work, and the SIL was offering all kinds of benefits. It was hard for other union leaders to not be coopted. Esteban disagreed with joining the SIL and in fact left the union and Walmart altogether. Yet others like Sandra have charismatic leadership that is able to move mountains. Nonetheless, they all have developed varying degrees of strategic capacity, militancy, and union democracy.

Unlike LTS, the independent unions have largely developed in response to a corrupt union, meaning that they have had to consistently fight against the employer, the corrupt union, and two other independent federations. For example, in contract negotiations they are pushing back on Walmart's bad faith bargaining (chapters 4 and 5), keeping the corrupt union from raiding their stores,[5] and at the same time trying to organize the other two labor federations to adopt some of their strategies to more effectively present a unified front to Walmart. In this regard they have had to work within a much more complicated political landscape than LTS. LTS has the good fortune of a highly centralized workforce and no competition from other unions.

Furthermore, these unions do not have the same structural power and political experience as LTS. Walmart stores are spread across Chile, and the two federations represent workers across the country. Additionally, they benefit from workforce concentration at the Híper Líder and Líder stores, but they also represent unions and workers in Walmart's fast growing small format stores, Ekono, that employ from eight to twenty workers. All of these features and circumstances have forced these unions into a more reactive than proactive position. They generally develop their strategy in response to what is directly happening on the shop floor, relying on the strength of their associational power to develop their symbolic disruptive capacity and, in a more limited way, their capacity to disrupt production. Although some of these unions have engaged in strikes, they have mostly relied on symbolic disruption to achieve their gains (see chapter 4). By contrast, the warehouse union has relied on the threat of disrupting production to achieve its gains.

Different Paths: Walmart's Warehouse and Retail Unions

Because of their different political histories, industry, leverage, and workplace issues, the independent retail and warehouse unions have each developed distinct ways of being. They collaborate and share strategies but

---

5. It is important to note that "raiding" in this context is different from the United States because unions in Chile do not have exclusive representation.

each one is unique in its organizational culture. The main characteristics of the warehouse union include a strong democratic tradition, political education, strategic capacity, and structural power—a combination I call strategic democracy. The main characteristics of the retail unions include strong associational power, strategic capacity, militancy, and formal democracy—a combination I call flexible militancy.

Strategic Democracy

The warehouse union maintained high levels of militancy initially and through its second contract. However, it has taken little militant action since its second contract, because its capacity to threaten action has given it enough power to achieve its goals without having to engage in militant action. The risk here is losing a tradition of militant culture. The longer the union is able to avoid direct action against Walmart because of its high level of membership participation and structural power, the more difficult it will be for the union to engage in militant action when the time requires it.

LTS is in a unique position, because it has a tremendous amount of leverage against Walmart. If the two central warehouses go on strike, Walmart Chile is essentially shut down, because it has no way of distributing goods to the stores. This situation gives the workers an incredible amount of structural power. In short, their capacity to disrupt production (and therefore obtain gains) comes from strong associational and structural power. Their associational power comes from the union's ability to devise good strategy and from union democracy, including a commitment to membership led decision making fostered by political education. Paradoxically, given the capacity for militant action afforded by its structural location, the union has prioritized political development and membership engagement over contract negotiations. This is not to say that it doesn't take contract negotiations seriously—it does—but on a daily basis the focus of the union is on building power. It is very clear that its strength in contract negotiations comes not only from its structural location in the industry but also (and perhaps even more importantly) from the strength and astuteness of its membership.

LTS's formal union structure includes eleven membership committees, including a women's committee, health and safety committee, newsletter committee, organizing and education committees, and the soccer team. The union also has a formal department steward structure where members volunteer to lead each department in the warehouse. The leadership is elected to three-year terms with a midterm membership vote of their confidence. If the membership is unhappy about the direction of the leadership in the midterm, they can vote them out of office. Membership meetings, called *asambleas*, are held every three months and have always had at least 80 percent attendance.

Political education is woven into the fabric of the union. In addition to setting up structures in the union to facilitate dialogue, debate, and participation, such as the committee and department steward structures, the union has also invested significant resources into leadership development for workers through the escuela sindical. Members are required to participate in the school's ten-week program at least once. These leadership workshops cover issues such as labor legislation, labor and working-class history, workplace rights, the labor code, and mapping production, a systematic way of understanding the flows of goods entering and leaving the warehouse and understanding what departments have the most strategic power (Jorge, executive committee member, interview 2011; Sindicato de Trabajadores Bodegas LTS 2010). As Rodrigo says, "unions exist not only to improve salaries, but also to improve working conditions, education, health, etc." (interview 2011). The union leadership realizes that sixty percent of its membership is comprised of young people who are inevitably consumer oriented. They believe participation in the escuela sindical will create greater levels of class-consciousness and union participation in general. As of 2013, over 400 workers had participated in the escuela and it has yielded incredible results.

The escuela sindical plays an instrumental role in socializing worker activists into the kinds of leaders who will promote union democracy, strategic thinking, and have a broader view of the role of labor in Chilean society. As such, one of the most important concepts that workers learn at the escuela sindical is Antonio Gramsci's notion of controlling production. Compelled by twentieth-century worker struggles in Turin, Gramsci believed that worker councils inside factories had true revolutionary potential, because these democratic forms, among other things, would give workers control over the productive process. Gramsci argues, "the existence of the council gives workers the direct responsibility of production, it draws them to improving the work, instills a conscious and voluntary discipline, creates the psychology of the producer, of the creator of history" (1919, 159). The union leadership has taken the concept of controlling production very seriously, and in the escuela sindical they jointly create knowledge with union members about the productive process in the warehouse. Historically, D&S often cheated workers, who didn't understand how their productivity bonuses were calculated.

As part of their training in the escuela sindical, workers learn how to map their workplace. This includes understanding the layout of the warehouse, who works in each section, strategic places for disruption inside the warehouse, the flow of goods to and from the warehouse, and worker output. Union members collect all this information about the warehouse, including data stored in the bosses' computers. This knowledge gives the union greater capacity to set minimum ranges for productivity bonuses and a better understanding of strategic points where it can disrupt production. As Sir Francis Bacon taught in 1597, "knowledge is power." In this case, knowledge of the internal workings of the warehouse is transformed into strategic leverage in contract negotiations. By mapping production, workers have both greater control over their own work lives and the ability to limit the surplus value being extracted from their labor. They have moved from being cheated from their wages to controlling the collective output of the warehouse and using these tools to demand more resources when management pressures them to produce more.

Through its path of strategic democracy, LTS has been able to create a union of innovation, leverage, and diffused knowledge. The leaders of the union have created an organization with unparalleled transparency and one in which the members are fully aware and engaged at all levels. Mapping production is particularly important, because it allows for both members and leaders to have equal expertise. As such, the vast majority of members who have been in the union for at least five years are capable of serving in leadership capacities, because they have vast knowledge and have been successfully developed. Therefore the union does not need to worry as much as other unions about leadership turnover, though in general there has been low leadership turnover at LTS. Furthermore, because LTS negotiates collective bargaining agreements instead of convenios, its leaders are protected by union immunity. Walmart management cannot decapitate the union by firing its leaders, because that would be an illegal action, but more importantly, even if key leaders were fired, there would be many strong candidates capable of accepting a leadership position, given the union's focus on leadership development.

Building a democratic union with strategic capacity, even before Walmart entered Chile, has spared LTS from Walmart's worst practices. In fact, the main issues that LTS has had with Walmart proper are subcontracting and the construction of a new non-union warehouse (under a different tax ID number). However, the union has been successful at keeping subcontracting to a minimum and helping the nonunion warehouse to successfully organize. To date, Walmart hasn't tried too many tricks with LTS, because it understands LTS's capacity for disrupting production. Furthermore, management is painfully aware that LTS's two warehouses are more efficient than its non-union warehouse. It is not in Walmart's interest to provoke this union. LTS has been fortunate that the initial strike was sufficient to build a strong union and maintain employer fear; however, this is not always the case for unions. Therefore figuring out when strikes might be effective or counterproductive can be a difficult decision.

Several case studies in Chile underscore the challenges of making the strategic decision to strike. Aravena and Nuñez's (2009) edited volume points to the reemergence of the strike as an important tactic in the revitalization of the labor movement, particularly among nontraditional workers. For example, Nuñez's (2009) case study of subcontracted copper workers highlights a series of successful actions and strikes between 2003 and 2007, some short, others longer, that finally led to cross-union collective bargaining. The labor struggle of the subcontracted copper workers supports Cohn's (1993) thesis that frequency of strikes is more important than winning or losing strikes in securing wage gains.

Building on protests and actions of 2003, subcontracted copper workers took advantage of high copper prices, record profits, and financial stability in the industry to force their employer—the Corporación Nacional del Cobre (CODELCO)—their employer, into negotiating an agreement during midterm elections in 2005. Unfortunately, neither CODELCO nor the contracting agency abided by that agreement, leading to a general strike in 2007. In the end it was this general strike, which included both symbolic disruption and stopping production, that ultimately forced the hand of management. Despite its victory, the union, through the labor ministry, was not able to force management to recognize these workers as permanent employees (Álvarez Vallejos 2009). Similarly, a forestry workers' strike in 2007 also led to sectoral bargaining and unprecedented gains in benefits and working conditions (Ruminot 2009).

Álvarez Vallejos (2009) case study of an extended strike in the salmon industries illustrates that even when these workers used many of the strategies of the copper workers' struggle, the political opportunities of the time had closed and, despite militant actions and significant disruption, these workers failed to force the hand of the employer.

In the case of Walmart warehouse workers, their 2006 strike to establish the first collective bargaining agreement was imperative for a number of reasons. First, only a strike would effectively challenge D&S's strong antiunionism and force it to negotiate. Second, union leaders understood that even with relatively small numbers they could significantly disrupt production. As a result of the strike, not only were they able to establish their capacity to disrupt production, they were able to negotiate their first contract, bringing many more workers into the ranks of the union. Now that they have firmly established their social power, it has been less important for them to go on strike, since the mere threat of strike is enough to force management to settle.

In short, the warehouse union's model of strategic democracy is based on its power to disrupt production, and this capacity is based on both the union's structural and associational powers. The strength of its associational power comes from union democracy, strategic capacity, and initial militancy.

Flexible Militancy

The independent retail unions are characterized by their flexible militancy. Like the warehouse union, they also have significant strategic capacity and union democracy, but their political histories, structural location, and workplace issues have driven the independent retail unions to construct a different kind of organizational culture. The independent retail unions understand that they do not have the same kind of structural power as the warehouse union. Therefore they have had to find a way to leverage the power they do have, the power to publicly shame the company. The two retail federations' social power comes from their capacity for symbolic disruption, and their capacity for symbolic disruption is based on their strong associational power, which comes in turn from their strategic capacity, union democracy, and ongoing militancy. Furthermore, the political and social landscape for organizing is quite different from LTS.

Retail workers are comprised of an entirely different demographic (mostly women) and set of leadership politics. The two independent retail federations that I worked with are confronted by a number of enemies: Walmart, the SIL company union, and two other existing federations. Owing to these circumstances they have developed a different practice. Because Chilean labor law allows them to have only enterprise-level unions and their membership is spread out across Santiago's dozens of Walmart stores, retail unions have had to be intentional about building strong store-level organizations. As a result, they tend to be much more responsive to daily conditions on the shop floor than LTS. Since LTS effectively controls production, it has fewer quarrels with Walmart in the daily functioning of the warehouse. By contrast, retail workers are harassed by management daily in terms of negotiating schedules, bathroom breaks, food quality, and workers' appearance, not to mention sexual and verbal harassment. Therefore, the retail unions have developed a more confrontational strategy based on daily experience.

Like LTS, these unions also have formal democratic structures, including committees, membership meetings, and elections. However, they have less widespread membership participation and political education. They also have different incentive structures than the warehouse union. For example, members are fined for not attending union meetings, and as a result they have high participation in membership meetings. The warehouse union, by contrast, does not fine members for absences but rather has built a union culture in which members want to attend meetings and understand the importance of their role in them. At the same time, attending the meetings is also easier for warehouse workers, because they have a stronger sense of collective identity from being concentrated in two workplaces rather than scattered across dozens.

Though the retail unions tend to do more work to incentivize participation, they nonetheless see the value in building strong leaders. For example, the Federación Autónoma has begun to employ the strategy of mapping production in retail stores. They engage in discussions with union leaders and members about all the different departments in the retail stores.

They push worker activists to understand the structural power they have in each departments. How can cashiers leverage power? Restockers? Fish mongers? Meat cutters? Bakers? Although workers don't have the power to shut down Walmart as a whole, they have discovered that the concept of "mapping production" helps them understand their workplace, and when something happens in a particular department they can use their knowledge and power in a delegation to the boss or some other action. Sandra used the following example,

> If a manager is giving a cashier a hard time about using the bathroom, and cashiers, as a class, understand that they have the power to disrupt sales and slow down lines, then that empowers them to act collectively and maybe all stand up and not work until the manager lets the one cashier go to the bathroom. (interview 2016)

This is a great example of how communication between the different autonomous unions leads to diffusion of knowledge and using that knowledge in creative ways. Additionally, a number of these union leaders have participated in the LTS escuela sindical, as well as other union schools affiliated with a number of universities in Santiago.

The retail unions have substantial strategic capacity, particularly as it relates to tactical innovations such as direct actions, delegations, and using legal resources. Furthermore, a number of these unions have participated in strike action. FENATRALID unions went on strike in 2006 (prior to Walmart's arrival), Ekono went on strike in 2011 (against Walmart), and Federación Autónoma took a strike vote in 2015 but did not go on strike. Furthermore, the Federación de Sindicatos Walmart, one of the other federations that I did not study also went on a strike right before Christmas in 2014, shutting down a number of important stores. Campusano's (2015) study on strikes in the service, finance, and commerce (including retail) sectors argues that while these sectors are responsible for 75 percent of legal strikes, most of these strikes are defensive. Interestingly in the case of Walmart retail workers, none of their strikes, except perhaps the Ekono strike, was a defensive strategy. Strikes were not used to regain rights workers had lost, instead they were used to solidify the union, bargain a first contract, or make new demands on the employer. Nonetheless, like the union leaders that Campusano interviewed, most Walmart retail union leaders agreed that strikes have lost their power since management won the right to replace striking workers, even when the strike is legal. Given the power imbalance between employers and workers, Urrutia (2015) forcefully argues that any labor law reform must eliminate the ability for employers to hire replacement workers, protect protest action as part of the strike itself, and provide real immunity to union leaders and workers involved in the conflict.

Although the retail unions do not have as much structural power as LTS, they do use the little structural power they have in creative ways. An example of their capacity for symbolic disruption is their use of the Chilean labor ministry's top ten list of antiunion firms, published twice a year. Employers on the list are fined and banned from government contracts for two years. Walmart consistently made the list between 2009 and 2014. The retail unions take this opportunity to educate customers about Walmart's antiunion practices, including chanting throughout the stores, flyering, and dropping banners. These federations and unions use their relationships with the public to create bad press for Walmart. This action, in turn, opens possibilities for the unions to mobilize their own memberships.

Conclusion

Since 2008, Chilean Walmart workers have been fighting against the odds. They are governed by a neoliberal state, with an antiquated labor code, and employed by the world's most antiunion corporation. Yet some of these unions have developed surprising and resilient organizations that are leading the charge against Walmart's behavior in Chile. The autonomous unions I worked with share the values of union democracy, strategic capacity, and militancy, whereas industry differences between the logistics and retail sectors and the development of their variable associational and structural power shape the social power that each of these unions has and has led each down a different path.

4

Strategic Democracy

Walmart's Warehouse Workers

Hoy siento una gran emoción. Por casi tres años he sido parte de
un gran cambio en la idea más legítima que pasa por mi corazón y
que es cambiar nuestra propia historia, no importa cuánto hemos
sufrido, cuántas amarguras, cuántas decepciones, lo importante es
creer que la unidad es una fuerza que construye y mientras exista
nadie puede detener, y a la empresa le digo: nos pueden robar nuestro
conocimiento, a veces nuestra dignidad y talvez muchas cosas más,
pero existe algo que jamás nos robaran, las ganas de luchar.

I feel great pride today. For almost three years I have been part of
a change in the most legitimate idea that passes through my heart.
Changing our own history. It doesn't matter how much we have
suffered, how much bitterness we have, how many disappointments
we have had. The important thing is that unity has the power to
build and while it exists nobody can stop us. To the company I say:
you can steal our knowledge and sometimes our dignity and maybe
many more things, but there is something you will never be able to
steal; our willingness to struggle.

—Rodrigo Villagra (2010; author translation)

My project in Chile was to understand how Chilean unions responded
to Walmart's entry into the country. After months of learning the political landscape of retail and warehouse unions in Chile, I was able to make
contact with the only Walmart warehouse workers' union at that time,
Logística, Transportación y Servicios (LTS).[1] My first encounter with the

---

1. Walmart's nonunion warehouse, DHL, opened in 2013.

union was with its part-time lawyer, Cristián González Santibáñez, who had been working with the union since it first organized in 2006. He invited me to the executive board meeting the following week.

We walked together across Santiago's downtown, through streets I had never encountered and ended up in front of an old warehouse that seemed closed. Cristián knocked on the metal gate, and one of the union members let us in. We walked into a room with fifteen men smoking and having *onces* (what we call teatime in Chile). Cristián introduced me, and they all invited me to have a seat at the table. I had many preconceived notions about what to expect from Chilean male unionists, based on my readings of Chilean labor history. The mainstream labor movement in Chile has historically been strongest in the manufacturing and mining sectors, though the public sector has played an important role in general strikes. Men have historically held the majority in union leadership positions and continue to do so, although women are increasing in numbers (Riquelme and Abarca 2015). In 2014, for the first time in its history, the national labor federation Central Unitaria de Trabajadores (CUT) representing the traditional labor movement finally proposed a "women's agenda," a set of policy proposals speaking directly to women's employment issues (Riquelme and Abarca 2015). In going into the meeting with LTS, I was fully expecting to encounter this kind of old unionism, especially in an industry as male-dominated as logistics/warehousing. However, this union was anything but typical. My stereotypical image was shattered when Jorge poured me a cup of tea and made me a butter and ham sandwich. This simple act broke the ice, and I was readily incorporated into the group as *la compañera,* a comrade.

My arrival had interrupted a vigorous conversation about Marx's notion of surplus value. Some of the older warehouse activists were explaining the concept to the newer leaders, who were somewhat skeptical. What followed for the next two hours was a nuanced and dynamic conversation on the fine points of Marxist theory and how it directly related to the organization of the shop floor, particularly in understanding how the boss controlled production bonuses. As the conversation flowed from what was happening on the shop floor to what was happening in the labor movement, I was particularly impressed by the gendered analysis communicated by the compañeros. Part of the conversation on the broader labor movement was about the flexibilization of labor and how that flexibility was particularly strong in female-dominated jobs. They also discussed the lack of women's leadership in their own union and how to change that. In all my years of U.S. union activism, I had never heard an executive committee debate the concept of surplus value on its own terms. I knew at that point that I had found a different kind of union.

The warehouse union has a strong capacity for disrupting production, a level of social power produced by its robust associational and structural power. LTS built associational power through its initial militancy, union democracy, and strategic capacity, but more recently its defining characteristics are union democracy and strategic capacity (see chapter 3). In this chapter, I take a closer look at strategic capacity and illustrate how it works on the shop floor level. But before analyzing how warehouse unionists have responded to Walmart, I want to step back and look at the working conditions and abuses that warehouse workers have faced under Walmart proper, because it is an important example of how Walmart pushes the limits of Chile's legal statutes.

Workplace Abuses and Employee Grievances

Given the many similarities in structure between D&S and Walmart, it is not at all surprising that LTS has the same issues with Walmart that it had with D&S (see chapter 2). In the pre-Walmart era and, in fact, before their successful drive to unionize, LTS workers suffered low wages and bad working conditions. They were frequently cheated out of their bonuses without understanding why their paychecks were so low. They had very few benefits and were subject to the whims of management; as Alberto, a member of the executive committee says, "if a supervisor liked you, you would get paid more at the end of the month. If a supervisor didn't like you or if you complained about unfair treatment, then your paycheck would be less" (interview 2011). Most important, their work environment was characterized by fear and intimidation. Gonzalo, another executive-committee member says, "I would get to work and immediately feel under surveillance. They would make us lock our things and not give them back until they declared the shift to be over. Sometimes we worked twenty hours" (interview 2011).

Under Walmart proper and with their union, workers have not had the same kinds of problems. Salaries are no longer low, and workers are not intimidated in the same way. Because they control production, they have a much clearer sense of what they have produced and what bonuses they can expect. Furthermore, rules and procedures have been formalized, making their workplace practices much more transparent. Walmart does try constantly to reduce the production bonus, but workers have successfully fought back on this issue. The one thing that has most changed between D&S and Walmart is the increased amount of subcontracted work. Walmart has benefitted from the flexibilization of labor in Chile, primarily through subcontracting, and has attempted to undermine the LTS union by using subcontracted work in two different ways.

First, in 2011 Walmart expanded subcontracted work inside the two existing warehouses. There had always been some subcontracted work in the warehouse, but it was minimal. For example, in 2008 the warehouse had only twenty subcontracted workers (González Santibáñez 2011). However, in 2011 Walmart laid off one hundred full-time LTS members and hired eighty subcontracted workers. This action created an uproar among workers, and the union immediately filed it as an unfair labor practice and demanded a meeting with management. After several months of bargaining over the matter and a legal battle in the courts, Walmart was forced to reinstate the laid off workers, and most importantly LTS won the right to incorporate the subcontracted workers into the organization.

The second, more problematic expansion of subcontracted workers was in the construction of a new Walmart warehouse. In 2011, Walmart started building a new warehouse in Lo Aguirre, not too far from the airport in Santiago. Construction was completed in 2012 and Walmart began hiring subcontracted workers through the German company DHL in 2013. As the nonunion Walmart warehouse was completed, LTS workers, especially at the main Walmart warehouse, started noticing changes, such as goods being moved from the main warehouse to the subcontracted warehouse and a remodeling to downsize the main LTS warehouse (Cristián, lawyer, interview 2013). While there is no concrete evidence that building a nonunion warehouse and shifting production to that warehouse were union-busting strategies, it seemed clear to the LTS leadership that these moves were intended to undermine the power they had built in the distribution system.

Strategic Democracy at LTS

To recap chapter 3, the model of unionism that most captures LTS is strategic democracy, which is characterized by strategic capacity, political education, and union democracy. Ganz (2000) sees strategic capacity as having three parts—heuristic processes, access to salient information, and motivation—which are influenced by leadership and organizational structure (see chapter 3). Ganz argues that the United Farm Workers Union beat the employer, the AFL-CIO, and the Teamsters because it had better strategic capacity than its opponents. Ganz states, "differences in strategic capacity were due to differences in leaders' life experience, networks, and repertoires of collective action and the deliberative processes, resource flows, and accountability structures of their organizations" (2000, 1005). He argues that organizations with greater strategic capacity have leadership teams comprised of insiders and outsiders, strong and weak ties in networks, and diverse sets of organizing experience and skills. Furthermore, these leadership teams are bolstered by organizations that have open deliberation, access to resources from varied constituencies, and a strong accountability structure. The LTS union fully meets these criteria. First, LTS has more access to salient information by having its pulse on the shop floor. Second, worker activists and the leadership body are all highly motivated, because they directly experienced the injustices of their workplace. Finally, the union is consistently learning from its methods and mistakes, thereby engaging in heuristic processes.

LTS also has a deep commitment to political education, particularly through its *escuela sindical* (union school). Participation in the escuela sindical ensures that all members, new and old, are schooled in a particular kind of unionism. Finally, LTS has a deep commitment to union democracy. For worker activists, as well as the leadership of the union, grassroots decision making is paramount. The union has formal union structures that facilitate democracy, but political education and leadership development play key roles in producing member activists who are consistently engaged in union work.

LTS has been able to effectively use strategic capacity, political education, and union democracy to build a grassroots union and leverage its power first against D&S and now against Walmart. As Ganz argues, "motivation enhances creativity by inspiring concentration, enthusiasm, risk taking, persistence, and learning. We think more critically when intensely interested in a problem, dissatisfied with the status quo, or experiencing a breach in our expectations" (2010, 12). LTS leaders were highly motivated, had salient knowledge, learned from their mistakes, benefitted from specific timing, and had vigorous deliberation, as illustrated in the epigraph to this chapter.

For all these reasons, the union had strategic capacity. However, its strategic capacity was also significantly enhanced by political education and union democracy, which aided their strategy thereby helping them to build strong associational power, which in turn allowed them to leverage their structural power. The union's commitment to political education, leadership development, and the democratic process sets it apart from other unions in the sector and, to some extent, some of the Walmart retail unions. The process of mapping production, where workers are trained by other workers and union activists to collect information on the flow of goods in and out of the warehouse, including computer data, is not only good strategy, but it is also about building a democratic union where knowledge is more equally distributed across the membership, and where members are trusted with their own capacity to act and make good decisions. Of course, LTS's strategic democracy took time to develop. In the early stages of its existence, it was primarily concerned with two things: obtaining a union and making sure that the union was different from labor unions embedded with management or the state.

The first test of LTS's strength was its 2006 strike. Shortly after being recognized as a union, LTS members voted to strike, because management was refusing to bargain. According to union leaders, D&S refused to believe that workers regarded LTS as a legitimate organization. In its arrogance, D&S missed the slow and deliberate covert organizing that workers engaged in for union recognition. Many workers, while not familiar with labor organizing, had some experience with antidictatorship organizing. D&S was completely blindsided. Good covert organizing allowed LTS to enlist enough members to form a legal union, but size alone was not enough to force management to bargain a contract with the union. The leaders of the nascent union understood that they could not succeed without a truly grassroots democratic union, one that could leverage power and force the hand of its employer. Given what they understood about the traditional Chilean trade union movement and its alliances with political parties, they believed it important to create an autonomous union. LTS member Sebastian says, "We wanted to break from tradition, and build a union that was not beholden to the Central Unitaria de Trabajadores or any of the political parties" (interview 2011). Most of all, union leadership understood that in order to have a successful strike they needed to have structures in place to encourage and formalize democratic decision making.

The union debated the merits of a strike strategy long and painfully for weeks before deciding to go on strike. Members agreed that they would not call a strike without consensus among all 200 of them. Once they achieved consensus, they made the strike public. LTS members remember the strike as simultaneously thrilling and terrifying. Over 200 workers went on strike, which caught the employer off guard, because it didn't think that the union was so well organized. However, at that time there were about 1,200 workers. The strikers had the difficult task of shutting down a warehouse where less than a quarter of the workers were actually on strike. They decided to use direct-action tactics to maximize impact. These tactics preceded similar disruptive tactics used in the 2007 strikes among subcontracted copper, forestry, and salmon workers that garnered national attention (Aravena and Nunez 2009). In his extensive study of strike activity and new forms of organization, Urrutia (2015) argues that in all the legal and illegal strikes he studied, unions incorporated direct-action tactics into the strike strategy. Thus, LTS was part of a new wave of unions working with multiple tactics as part of their organizing strategy.

Union member José describes the first few hours of the strike,

> We agreed to meet before the first shift. We arrived at six in the morning and our first action was to block the entrance to the company with banners and chains. Our idea was not to let anyone in or out. That day, the night shift was at the company almost thirty hours because we wouldn't let them leave and the people not on strike couldn't go inside. Trucks with goods were not allowed into the warehouse and trucks loaded with goods were not allowed out. (LTS 2010)

The strikers maintained considerable control of the warehouse for the first two to three days. Then the police arrived. Despite police attacks, workers held strong. For three additional days they stopped the one hundred and twenty trucks that left the warehouse daily to distribute goods to supermarkets. The strikers had previously built relationships with some of the retail-worker unions and were receiving word that their strike was creating havoc in the supermarkets because they weren't receiving merchandise.

The company in conjunction with the police continued harassing and repressing workers. By the end of the first week of the strike, D&S had also begun to hire strikebreakers (González Santibáñez 2011). The strikers would have to diversify their tactics. The large group divided into smaller, more militant strategic-action teams, several of which began to tamper with the company's electrical system and generators. This tactic put the company in a weak position, because half the warehouse relies on refrigeration to preserve millions of dollars' worth of perishable food products. The more the company fought back, the more the strikers fought back. After three weeks of intense direct action and militant fighting, the company agreed to meet with the union and bargain in good faith (González Santibáñez 2011). Ultimately the strike succeeded because of the effective strategy that workers developed over the course of the month long action. Workers started out with a picket line, then quickly moved to chaining themselves around the entrance to the warehouse and blocking distribution trucks. When they lost control over that, they diversified their tactics and deployed small, strategic teams to tamper with the warehouse's electrical system. At the same time they were building solidarity and coalition with retail workers who informed them that their strategy was working. In the 2006 strike we see the development of the organization's strategic capacity. The strike action itself provided political education, while union democracy was still a nascent concept.

Shortly after the end of the strike, union membership exploded. The union wanted to grow, but some of the workers who went on strike felt a great deal of resentment toward the workers who crossed the picket line. How would the union leadership reconcile workers who went on strike and those who didn't? This question marked a crucial moment in LTS history. Again, the union faced a difficult strategic decision. Raul, a shop floor steward, remembers vigorous debate about whether the strikebreakers should be allowed to be in the union. In the end, LTS chose to incorporate these workers and build its union capacity. It was at that moment that the union really understood the value of prioritizing political education (Jorge, interview 2011). The workers who went on strike had been politicized in the context of the strike and political struggle. They recognized management's offensive, started understanding tactical innovation and strategy, and benefitted from constant discussion and debate on the picket line and after hours. However, the nonstriking workers did not have the benefit of having gone through this political process, instead they witnessed it from afar. For the LTS leadership it was imperative to offer the new members (at that point a vast majority of the union) political education in order to build a union with all workers having full access to information, discussion, and debate. As a result of the growing membership and tensions between new members and original strikers, the union decided to create its school.

Even though the union had only negotiated a modest contract (see below), the primary purpose of the strike had been to force management to collectively bargain and to build the LTS union. In this regard it succeeded, and even though the economic gains were not significant, workers got their first sense of their true power. The success of the strike and the incorporation of many new members into the ranks of the union helped the union along its path to strategic democracy. LTS succeeded with D&S and then Walmart because at each stage in its development the union capitalized on different sources of power. In the beginning, LTS spent significant time developing its shop floor organization. It followed up with a unique legal strategy and having luck with timing for its 2008 contract. Subsequent contract negotiations have succeeded without strike threat because of the strong and democratic shop floor organization that LTS has built. In some ways, union members have made themselves indispensable to Walmart.

Shop Floor Organization

One of the greatest feats that came out of the 2006 strike was the one-on-one organizing strategy that the union adopted. It understood that in order to have the greatest power, to be truly democratic, and to develop leadership, it had to reach every single person in the warehouse. In the post-strike period, the LTS union spent significant time developing its committee structure, political education, and leadership development. The union set up a shop steward structure, an organizing committee, a health and safety committee, and a newsletter committee. Later it added the welfare fund, women's committee, cultural committee, and soccer team (Villagra, interview 2011). During this period new leaders emerged and members began to take seriously what full participation in their union meant. Besides establishing the union school, members met on a regular basis and wrote and distributed newsletters in an underground way (they had not earned the contractual right to distribute materials at that point).

In the months after the strike the union also formalized its program for political development and socialization. Workers who had been radicalized through the process of the strike recognized the importance of political education for the strength of their union. In addition to the escuela sindical, the union leadership decided to hold a mass membership meeting every three months. At first, only about 50 percent of the membership participated in the meetings, so shop stewards started organizing workers in their areas to attend. By the time of my arrival in Santiago in 2011, it was standard for over eighty percent of workers to come to the membership meetings. I was invited to attend the May 2011 membership meeting. In all my years in the labor movement, I had never experienced a membership meeting like this. First off, union activists told me the meeting was in a theater. I immediately envisioned a movie theater, but they meant a performing arts theater. I found this odd, but then Cristián explained that the membership always met in a theater because it was the only space that could accommodate 1,500 workers. As it turns out, Santiago has dozens of old theaters that are largely out of use, so it is relatively inexpensive to rent them out for union events. I doubted that so many members would come to the meeting, but they did. At nine in the morning on a Sunday, I watched as hundreds of workers and many of their families came to attend the meeting. The meeting lasted until 1 p.m. and included a Mapuche cultural performance, a discussion of the agenda, and a vote on how to distribute the newly earned productivity bonus. The president of the union started by linking the struggle of the Mapuches (one of Chile's few indigenous groups) to the struggle for justice at work. He then asked if anyone had anything to add to the agenda. A few minor issues were added. This opener was followed by a two-hour conversation about a recently settled lawsuit against Walmart in which the union was given back wages on a productivity bonus that Walmart had underpaid. Per the settlement, Walmart deposited the back wages (about US$20,000) into the union's bank account. The union's executive board could have made the decision on how to distribute the funds, or it could have made a recommendation to the membership, but because there was not consensus among the executive board members, they decided that it would be a good opportunity for the membership to have the conversation as a whole and make the final decision on how to distribute the funds. The main question was whether to distribute the money among all union members or only to workers who had been members in 2009/10.

A serious discussion with members took place and addressed the costs and benefits of each approach. Members held microphones and passed them around the entire theater so that everyone was heard. Members were passionate about the issue and felt strongly on both sides, but everyone worked hard to be civil and even-tempered. Some members argued that it was not fair for new members to receive the bonus, because they had not participated in the fight. They felt like the bonus should be distributed among only those members who had struggled. Many arguing this position feared that if new members received the bonus without having to work for it, they would be less inclined to take risks and come to expect benefits without participating in union struggles. Other members argued that for the sake of unity, the bonus should be distributed to all members and that sharing it would show new members the level of solidarity in the union. They also argued that there would be plenty of opportunities for new members to participate in struggles around different issues. Yet other members were neutral on the matter and asked practical questions about how the distribution of funds would work.

Members of the executive board did not speak on the issue until all other worker leaders had an opportunity to speak. When executive board members finally spoke, they tended to present the costs and benefits of each approach, rather than simply presenting their own positions. Eventually, after a full discussion was aired, the meeting facilitator called for a vote by secret ballot, reminding members that regardless of the vote's outcome, unity was their strength. In the end, a strong majority of members (79 percent) voted in favor of giving a percentage of the productivity bonus to new members. I later learned that this was the outcome the executive committee had hoped for (Andres, executive committee, 2011). Executive committee member Andres said, "we had no way of knowing how the membership would vote. We could only rely on the political education that we've developed, which has emphasized the collective over the individual" (Andres, executive committee, 2011).

The membership meeting serves several purposes. First, it gives the union a forum to discuss and debate major decisions. This level of open discussion, while at times cumbersome, gives the members a sense of their collective power. The agenda is sent to all members ahead of time, and members are free to add to the agenda at the meeting itself. Second, the membership meeting gives members a chance to physically see their power. In the warehouse they are divided into their small subareas, but in the membership meeting they see the sheer numbers of their collective unity. I cannot describe in words how powerful it felt, even as an outsider, to see an entire theater filling with hundreds of workers and their families. Third, the membership meeting gives the union the opportunity to provide some cultural and political education. In this particular meeting it was the Mapuche history as told though dance. The performance, which lasted about thirty minutes, was produced and performed by members of the union (the cultural committee). Finally, by inviting the families of workers, the meeting plays a key role in community socialization. The meeting is an event. Even though they can't vote on the issues at hand, workers' families develop an important sense of participating in the life of the union and being involved in the serious decision making that happens. The meeting gives the children of these workers the opportunity to witness firsthand what it means to be a union member.

Legal Strategy

In the period after the 2006 strike and before the 2008 contract negotiations, worker activists began to feel a great deal of frustration about their workplace. They had gained a lot of dignity on the job, but their wages continued to be low and they had no union office, no access to a bulletin board on the shop floor for announcements, and no reassigned time to do the work of running the union. Furthermore, they expressed a variety of health and safety concerns. Around this time they started developing their legal strategy in earnest. They knew that the 2008 contract negotiations would not be easy. The executive committee decided that it would be beneficial for worker activists to establish a record of health and safety and labor law violations. The union would use this record to make arguments over the course of the contract negotiations. Cristián González Santibáñez helped the union to develop its legal strategy, and the union trained workers in the basics of labor law, so that they could identify problems on the shop floor. In the months that ensued, the union consistently filed claims with the labor inspectorate and won on issues of contract violations, productivity bonuses, and health and safety concerns around the amount of time workers spent in the refrigerated sections of the warehouse (Cristián, lawyer, interview 2011). This kind of legal strategy has become more prevalent in Chile in the post-dictatorship period. During Bachelet's first term she appointed a decidedly pro-labor head of the labor inspectorate. Given the little power that unions have under Chilean labor law, one strategy has been to take grievances to the courts instead of the streets in the form of strikes and other direct action. Since the courts in Bachelet's first term were particularly favorable to workers, this strategy helped workers not only to defend their existing rights but also to extend their rights (Gutierrez Crocco 2015). However, the legal strategy does not come without costs. In particular, it can cause unions to rely too much on the courts instead of building power in their own ranks (Gutierrez Crocco 2015; Stillerman 2004). Furthermore, it can be a risky strategy that at the end of the day favors management over workers (Gutierrez Crocco 2015; Stillerman 2004).

Relying exclusively on a legal strategy undoubtedly has serious limitations, whereas a legal strategy combined with deep organizing and militancy has more chances of success. LTS's legal strategy was always only one aspect of the work to which it had committed. Union leaders did not see it as a substitute. Furthermore, union leaders recognized early on that there was something fishy happening with D&S, because the company seemed to be overreacting to the grievances that were being filed with the labor inspectorate. Shortly before contract negotiations began in 2008, union activists noticed that D&S wanted to settle quickly. Repeatedly D&S asked the union to bring its concerns directly to the company and said it would handle the legal issues outside of formal structures. It was not until much later, after the contract had been negotiated, that the union understood that D&S was nervous because it had been in conversations with Walmart about selling a majority of shares to the U.S. corporation.

External Forces

The union did not realize it until later, but the sale of D&S to Walmart had presented it with a significant political opportunity. Walmart's success in Chile hinged on abiding by Chilean laws, including accepting unions. Given its history in the United States, it would not have been prudent for Walmart to purchase a Chilean company embroiled in labor scandals. Conversely, Walmart was not interested in buying a company where the union was too strong. Therefore, D&S had to demonstrate that it did not have significant conflicts (i.e., lawsuits) and a track record of union peace. No other labor contracts expired in 2008 during the Walmart and D&S negotiations, except for LTS's. The warehouse workers had no idea that they had more leverage than usual (Cristián, lawyer, interview 2011).

The LTS union first heard about the potential Walmart purchase during the 2008 contract negotiations and quickly grasped the situation (Rodrigo, president, interview 2011). The threat of a strike, especially like the one in 2006, would be disastrous for the delicate negotiations between Walmart and D&S. D&S knew it had to deliver labor peace. The solution seemed obvious: agree to most of the union's demands in this round of negotiations and hand the problem over to Walmart (Rodrigo, interview 2011).

The success of the union in the poststrike period makes sense. LTS spent substantial energy building its union from the bottom up by focusing on union democracy, militancy, and strategic capacity, thereby creating strong associational power. As a result of its strong associational power, the union was able to leverage its structural power by way of a strike threat. The negotiations between D&S and Walmart created a political opportunity that forced the employer to meet the workers' contract demands. I elaborate on the gains earned in the contract below, but how do we explain LTS's continued success under Walmart proper? To this I turn next.

Bread-and-Butter Wins

The 2006 LTS contract did not yield many bread-and-butter gains. Workers won a modest wage increase and some benefits, but the real win in that negotiation was their consolidation as a union and setting up structures to build power. The 2008 contract was an entirely different story, owing to the leverage of the impending sale of D&S to Walmart and the union's increased membership. With over one thousand members, the union received very different treatment from the company than it had in 2006; the union had more than tripled its membership.

In 2008, the union won a 15 percent wage increase and a collective productivity bonus, the biggest innovation in the contract. D&S had initially offered an individual productivity bonus once workers had achieved 75 percent of the production goal. Union leaders debated the merits of an individual productivity bonus. They were used to being paid (albeit unreliably) an individual productivity bonus, and many of them did not like that it forced competition between workers. They felt that now that they were unionized it no longer made sense to compete with one another. Workers in Stillerman's (2004) case study also pointed to the dangers of individual productivity bonuses because they played into the individualism promoted by neoliberal policies. Of course D&S was interested in maintaining the individual productivity bonus because it undermines class solidarity while profiting the company. Under this model, workers are forced to compete with each other in order to maximize individual gains, which yields maximum productivity for employers while undermining worker solidarity (Burawoy 1979). In this instance the union leadership and rank-and-file workers agreed that individual productivity bonuses would undermine the work of the union. When workers had received individual bonuses in the past, and keeping track of them was hard. Ignacio recalls, "the company used to use these bonuses to make us feel special, but we didn't understand how they worked, so we didn't realize when we were being cheated" (executive committee member, interview 2011). The bonus appeared to be a benefit when in fact it was an illusion by which management consistently cheated workers.

The union came up with the idea of pushing for a collective productivity bonus that would motivate workers to work together. Generally the employer sets the productivity level, usually 100 percent for individual workers. However, in the 2008 negotiations, the union was very clear that it would not agree to a productivity bonus above 75 percent, and that it had to be collectively achieved. The union recognized that labor education about the productivity bonus was imperative to not break the union. At the escuela sindical and on the shop floor workers learned that they should never go beyond the 75 percent productivity mark, even when they can, because it is simply free labor to the company. The level of productivity set in the contract was a very important discussion among the membership. It forced them to collectively think about health and safety concerns, how the level of productivity works in the different subdivisions of the factory, and most importantly how working together benefits everyone rather than individuals (Rodrigo, interview 2011).

In addition to the collective productivity bonus, workers also won the right to two union offices in each of the warehouses, plus a union office in downtown Santiago, all paid for by management. The union president obtained release time from his job for his union work, and the bargaining team also won release time from work in order to bargain the contract. In addition, two members of the executive board were also given release time to carry out the work of the union. These two additional release time members are rotating and work on special projects. Everyone else on the executive board and in the union works a full-time shift in addition to their union work. Workers also made gains such as an improved transportation benefit, which came in two different forms. According to the 2008 contract, workers received more money to take public transportation to work, and second, the company hired more busses to pick workers up in different neighborhoods and bring them to the warehouses. The additional busses were especially important for workers living on the outskirts of Santiago, with no easy access to public transportation. The 2008 contract also formalized hours worked on major holidays such as Christmas, Easter, and Chilean Independence Day.

The 2011 contract was the first one negotiated with Walmart proper. Workers won an unprecedented 30 percent wage increase. This new wage increase, along with a renegotiated productivity bonus, makes the Walmart warehouse workers among the highest paid warehouse workers in Chile. In fact, many of the most senior Walmart warehouse workers earn a higher monthly wage than subcontracted immigrant Walmart warehouse workers in the United States. LTS members who have worked for five years earn a base wage of US$600 per month and a collective productivity bonus of US$175 per month (Ignacio, interview 2011). With the addition of other bonuses, union members with seniority earn over US$1,000 per month. Subcontracted immigrant workers at Walmart's warehouses in the United States earn minimum wage and often cannot obtain full-time jobs.

On average they work twenty to thirty hours a week, which amounts to between US$640 and US$960 per month (Sanjay, staff Warehouse Workers United, interview 2012).

In 2013 LTS represented over 1,800 warehouse workers in two of the three main Walmart warehouses in Santiago. Wages tripled between 2006 and 2013 and benefits were dramatically expanded. Even in its negotiation with Walmart proper, the union made unprecedented gains.

Respect and Dignity on the Job

In addition to all the concrete wage and benefit increases workers at the LTS warehouse have gained, they have made huge strides in achieving dignity on the job. The union culture inside the warehouse is unlike any I have seen anywhere in the United States. At most U.S. factories I had entered legally or illegally in my capacity as a union organizer, I was escorted off of company grounds. I expected this to happen at the LTS warehouse, especially because it is a heavily secured fortress. Walmart's headquarters are in the front of the property and the largest of the two LTS warehouses is in the back. In order to drive me to the warehouse Cristián had to get through two security checkpoints. At each he simply said I was with the union. At the main entrance there is a third security checkpoint where three union leaders were waiting to meet us. Once again, when security asked who I was and what I was doing in the warehouse, LTS members said, "she is a friend of the union" and walked right past security. As I was putting on my safety shoes, one of the worker activists told us that security had alerted management about my visit and management had asked why I was let into the warehouse without the company's permission. The union president got on the phone and said, "we do not need your permission to bring our guest into the warehouse." Management backed down and asked the president to give them a heads up in the future, if it was not inconvenient. I have never seen management back down in the way that Walmart backed down in Chile.

As the three worker activists led me through the warehouse we were constantly greeted by other union members who wanted to show us their area and tell us about the main issues they were confronting on the job. Some talked about improvements in health and safety equipment; others talked about the new technology in the warehouse. They often stood and spoke to us for fifteen to twenty minutes. They expressed no concern that management was going to tell them to get back to work, or that there would be reprisals for speaking to us. In fact, when I asked if they were worried that management was going to reprimand them for taking a break without permission, one of the workers responded, "five years ago, I would have never stopped to talk to you, but now what are they going to say? We have a union. We are the most productive workers they have ever had. I do my work, so I can stop whenever I want" (informal interview 2012). Workers showed pride not only in their union accomplishments but also in the quality of their work. Now that working conditions in the warehouse had improved, many workers commented that they enjoyed their work much more than they had formerly.

As we walked through the warehouse, I noticed bulletin boards with union information about upcoming committee meetings, general meetings, and the escuela sindical displayed prominently in many key areas. The two union offices were also filled to capacity with worker leaders engaging in the daily aspects of union work, such as filing grievances and managing the welfare fund. Members were also busy writing the union newsletter and updating the website. The energy was incredible compared to two nonunion warehouses in southern California that I visited in 2009.

Workplace Control

Their systematized control of production is a significant part of why workers can hold their heads high in the warehouse. Mapping production gives them control over the production process, and knowing exactly what arrives and leaves the warehouse, how fast they are operating, and when to strategically slow down, gives warehouse workers substantial power (see chapter 3).

Without the kinds of democratic structures built into the everyday practices of the union, workers would not be able to wield this power effectively. Mapping production, having a union office in each of the warehouses, and having a weekly union newsletter, website, and bulletin boards throughout the warehouse all contribute to the vibrancy and success of the union. The strategy and the democratic structures work together to ensure success. This is more evident than in the covert organizing LTS has engaged in with respect to the new subcontracted Walmart warehouse mentioned in the beginning of the chapter.

As of 2013 Walmart claimed that its new warehouse was fully functional (Walmart 2013). But through the process of mapping production workers at the other two warehouses have determined that the new, subcontracted warehouse has actually been disastrous for Walmart. At first, workers began documenting the shift in flows away from the two warehouses in Santiago to the new warehouse, but soon they also started hearing reports from the supermarkets that goods arriving from the new warehouse were often severely damaged. During contract negotiations, union leaders were able to collect financial data from Walmart itself, which showed that Walmart was losing over US$600,000 per month in the subcontracted factory (Cristián, lawyer, interview, 2013). While Walmart struggled to understand why its new super high-tech warehouse with subcontracted workers was so grossly underperforming, it made perfect sense to the unionized workers at LTS. The subcontracted warehouse workers at the new warehouse lacked the skills, experience, and expertise to move goods at the level of efficiency that the unionized workers could. Furthermore, the subcontracted workers were so poorly paid that there was rapid turnover of employees. By late 2013, Walmart had to increasingly shift production away from the new warehouse and back into the two unionized plants (Cristián, interview, 2013). Walmart seems to understand the price of skilled labor, but that hasn't kept the corporation from trying to undermine the union and cut costs. Without mapping production daily, workers would have never understood the movement of goods to and from the new warehouse. In the 2013 negotiations of productivity bonuses, the union used the information it had gathered about losses at the new warehouse to demand higher bonuses for workers at the two unionized warehouses.

Furthermore, in 2013 members of the executive board did some reconnaissance to obtain information about the subcontracted workers at the new warehouse. A subcommittee made contacts and told the subcontracted warehouse workers about the other two warehouses and the benefits they had successfully bargained. Because it has a different tax ID code from LTS, per the Chilean labor code LTS cannot formally organize the new warehouse. However, in 2014 LTS workers worked with the subcontracted workers to help them form their own union. The new

DHL union bargained its first contract in mid-2016. Another way LTS has strategically located itself is in their initial participation in the Consejo de Trabajadores Walmart Chile.

Consejo de Trabajadores Walmart Chile

Besides helping subcontracted workers to form a union of their own, another way LTS has strategically located itself is in its initial participation in the Consejo de Trabajadores Walmart Chile (Walmart Chile Workers Council), founded in 2011. The Consejo was made up of LTS plus two independent Walmart retail union federations and their affiliates, including union locals representing workers at Lider, Lider Express, Ekono, and Acuenta. The Consejo marks the second attempt by these groups to unite into a cohesive organization that meets on a regular basis, engages in collective projects, and builds solidarity among like-minded Walmart unions in Chile. While the Consejo's cohesiveness has fluctuated, it has done useful work and allowed its participants to share key information. While I was in Chile, the Consejo was meeting on a weekly basis. Members shared what was happening inside their unions, what kinds of information Walmart provided them, and successful and unsuccessful strategies around organizing and grievances. They also developed joint statements for the local unions to discuss, debate, and sign. For example, in 2012 the Lider Valdivia was in contract negotiations and presented with a 0 percent economic offer. The Consejo started a pressure campaign and everyone signed a petition to Walmart headquarters. Pressure from the Consejo and a strike threat from the members in Valdivia led to a positive outcome for that local. In the end, despite being located in the south of Chile, it was able to get the same wages and bonuses as Lider stores in Santiago. According to the Consejo, Walmart management was taken aback when it received a petition regarding a store in Valdivia. It did not realize that the networks reached across the country.

At its highpoint, the Consejo served as a conduit for debate and distribution of ideas. LTS played a significant role in the Consejo and many LTS ideas were diffused through the Consejo into the various Walmart store-level unions. Unfortunately, in 2012 some tensions arose between LTS and retail unions around participation and cooperation between the United

Food and Commercial Workers Union, Change to Win Labor Federation, UNI Global Union, and the Chilean unions. As a result, LTS formally left the group, although it continues to work with unions who want to work with it. Leaving the Consejo has been one of the greatest leadership failures of the LTS union. It has lost the respect of some of the locals, which could hurt LTS in future strikes. Perhaps more importantly it has lost the opportunity to diffuse its very good ideas through the group. The LTS has lost in terms of organizational dynamism, and the Consejo has lost a valuable resource. While the Consejo continues to meet, it does so on an ad hoc basis.

Conclusion

LTS has consistently and effectively used good strategy, while building and maintaining a democratic union that engages in serious political education and leadership development. In each of its contract negotiations, LTS developed its strategic capacity, political education, and union democracy. Table 4.1 summarizes LTS's tactics and the results they yielded in each contract negotiation.

TABLE 4.1. LTS's tactics and results in contract negotiations

Year	Tactics	Wins	Concessions
2006	One-month strike, human chain, sabotage (electrical tampering), locking themselves inside warehouse, delegations to management	Negotiated first contract, received modest pay increase and transportation benefit, allowed to have a bulletin board	None
2008	Legal strategy, strike threat, mapping production, leveraging D&S sale to Walmart	15 percent pay increase, two union offices in warehouses and a union office in downtown Santiago, release time for president and bargaining team, expansion of bulletin board, collective productivity bonus	None
2011	Legal strategy, mapping production	30 percent wage increase	None
2013 (bonus only)	Mapping production	Increase in collective productivity bonus	Increase in productivity goal from 75 to 90 percent

Whereas the first contract was weak, as the union developed strategic democracy, contracts exponentially improved, until 2013. In 2013, we see a higher productivity bonus, but the union was forced to concede on the level of productivity.

LTS has been most successful in building a union culture on the shop floor that has yielded substantial economic benefits for its members. It learned to leverage its structural power early on and has maintained that power. However, it has not seriously engaged in militant action since the 2008 contract negotiations. Perhaps this disuse is simply because it has been able to leverage its power effectively, but it might also represent a dangerous complacency, given how relentless Walmart is as an employer.

5

The Flexible Militancy of Walmart Retail Workers

Retail workers at Walmart Chile tend to be young working-class women, with high school degrees and little labor market experience. Stecher (2012) points out in his work on the Chilean retail industry that many women who worked as domestics are now in the retail industry because it offers more freedom and flexibility than domestic work, and the pay and benefits are comparable. Sandra Neida, whose mother worked as a domestic worker for the Ibáñez family, owners of D&S, is a good example of the kind of worker at Walmart Chile. She told me in a 2011 interview how she grew up to become president of the Matucana local and the Federación Autónoma:

> I come from a very humble family. My father worked at the farmers market and my mother was a domestic worker for the Ibáñez family. Growing up I frequently helped her out at the Ibáñez house. Eventually the Ibáñez's began to notice how industrious I was. As a favor to my mother they offered me a job at one of the Líder stores. This was our ticket out of poverty.

I was very grateful for the opportunity to work in retail rather than domestic service. But the more I worked, the more I saw abuses, so I got involved in the union. At that time I was an activist in the Interempresa union, but then I broke out of that when I recognized that the union leader didn't really want to fight for the rights of workers. So here I am now, the president of my own local union and the president of the Federation of Autonomous Unions. Imagine all the trouble I've caused for the Ibáñez's.

Workplace Abuses

The story of abuses on the retail side of Walmart Chile is not dissimilar to Walmart's operations in the United States or the rest of the world. Despite assurances that it would respect unions and workers in Chile, Walmart has abused workers in various ways, violated the labor code, or pushed the law to its limits. Although there are too many stories to detail in one chapter, I hope to bring to life some of the most egregious transgressions in the areas of human rights, fundamental rights, wages, hours, breaks, and antiunionism.

Human Rights

Long before Walmart's acquisition of D&S, the latter hired Sergio Díaz as director of the Assets Protection department (otherwise known as Internal Security or Theft department). According to *La Nación,* a Chilean newspaper, and various accounts by workers themselves, Díaz was an ex-agent of the Central Nacional de Informaciones (CNI)[1] and had already been convicted of three counts of torture committed during the dictatorship ("El 'Sucio de DyS' " 2011). During his time at D&S he used the military handbook on interrogations to train his staff. Workers were terrified of Díaz, who relied on techniques frequently employed in secret police interrogations, including repeatedly asking questions that had already been answered, questioning employees about how nervous they felt, and blaming them for theft and forcing confession (Cristián, lawyer, interview, 2011). Walmart employed Díaz until 2010.

---

1. The CNI in Chile combined the functions of the U.S. CIA, FBI, and Secret Service.

On August 5, 2009, Andrea (a receptionist) and Crisóstomo (in-store manager of groceries) were accused of theft at a Walmart store. They were brought to Walmart headquarters on August 12 and locked in an interrogation room, where they could not see out, but people passing by could see them. Díaz interviewed each worker separately for over two hours and interviewed the store security managers and assistant managers, also in the locked interrogation room. Workers and managers essentially spent the day in this security office, waiting to be interviewed or waiting to be released. Díaz asked Andrea about her children and what would happen to them if she were gone. This vague threat alluded to her potential disappearance, thereby leaving her children motherless. Díaz told both workers that they would not be fired from their jobs, but that if they talked to anyone outside of Walmart (about the interview), then they would be fired for revealing confidential information. During this interrogation they had no access to lawyers or union representatives. Díaz extracted forced confessions from the two Walmart workers. Andrea and Crisóstomo went back to work, but their working environment was difficult. Other workers and managers treated them with fear, hostility, and zero faith. They were both fired three weeks later.

This story, derived from the retail union's legal adviser and court documents, reveals the dangerous precedent set by D&S and subsequently followed by Walmart. These workers were subjected to fear tactics and intimidation in the most abusive sense, especially given that they had lived through the dictatorship and had felt firsthand the violation of their human rights during the 1970s and 1980s. Ironically, this conduct contradicts Walmart's "Ethics Manual," which claims that the employer wants to create a workplace that is "honest, just, and respectful" (Walmart 2011). Furthermore, the manual states,

> We believe in maintaining a workplace environment free of violence or threats of violence. This means that we will not tolerate inappropriate language, gestures, threats of violence or actual physical violence. This kind of behavior creates hostile working conditions and violates the first of the three basic principles: Respect for the Person. (Walmart 2011, 12; author translation)

Military style interrogation tactics that rely on threats clearly create a hostile work environment. Only in this case the threats were not being perpetrated by another employee, but by the highest leadership of Walmart in Chile. Thus, while the ethics handbook says one thing, in reality Walmart exercises a different practice. Furthermore, after Díaz's employment was terminated in 2010, Walmart replaced him with Alfredo Saint Jean Junior, the son of an officer in the Argentine military during the dictatorship of José Rafael Videla (1976–13), who had also been convicted of human rights violations.

Fundamental Rights

Chile has a relatively strong labor code on what it calls fundamental rights. These include, "the right to life and physical integrity, the right to private communications, the right to honor, conscience and religion, free speech, freedom to enter into employment contracts, and freedom from sexual harassment" (Rosado Marzán 2010, 505). In addition, the fundamental rights clause of the labor code guarantees freedom to choose a union and the right to collectively bargain, the right to nondiscrimination, and freedom from employer reprisals (Dirección del Trabajo 2014, 1). In the following examples the right to honor and nondiscrimination became particularly important.

In 2010 a cashier named Mauricio Gomez grew a beard. A customer service manager told him to shave off his beard because it made him look indigent and might turn away customers. He cited a new Walmart employee manual that dictated how Walmart employees should look. Employees must appear well groomed. Women with painted nails can only wear red nail polish, not bright colors such as hot pink. Women with long hair should wear it in a ponytail. Mauricio was shocked; "I couldn't believe these words came out of the manager's mouth. I have never had this kind of experience" (Mauricio, worker, interview, 2011). Lorena, a union leader, commented, "it reminded me of the dictatorship, when Pinochet decided women couldn't wear pants" (interview 2011). Workers and union leaders were appalled that these were new company policies.

In the same week, the same manager told Sandra Neida that she should get rid of her rattail hairstyle—a short-cropped haircut, with a long, tail-like piece of hair growing from the nape of the neck—because it was offensive to clients. Although the attack was not specifically homophobic, the manager clearly objected to her gender presentation. Sandra said, "I understand that people who work with food, like in the bakery or butcher, need to be careful with their hair. That's about hygiene, but I'm a cashier. It's ridiculous. . . . This kind of thing never happened at D&S" (Sandra, president of Federación Autónoma, interview, 2011).

Both Mauricio and Sandra went to talk to their union representatives, and the local union launched a "Respect at Work" campaign. Other union members were indignant that a transnational corporation was coming into their country and imposing its own cultural values about appearance. Out of the organizing it emerged that other Walmart workers were also being harassed about their appearances. Laura Franco, a Walmart employee in another city, complained, "they [store managers] have been giving me a hard time about wearing all the same color. When I wear purple, I like to wear it head to toe" (interview 2011). In Chile all Walmart workers wear uniforms. More often than not workers see this as a benefit, since the company provides them several outfits for different seasons free of charge. This means that workers do not have to spend their own wages on clothing for work. In fact, when Ekono-Walmart workers first started organizing their stores, this was one of the workers' most important demands, because they only received a vest, instead of a full uniform from the company.

All three examples of attacks on an individual's appearance support the literature on employer or corporate control over bodies at work (Adkins 1995; Casanova 2011, 2013; McDowell 2009; Tyler and Hancock 2001; Wolkowitz 2006). Wolkowitz argues that Tyler and Hancock (2001) and Adkins (1995) particularly emphasize the "economic value of heterosexualized gender performance to the employer in attracting customers and providing them with the services they enjoy" (2006: 83). Walmart wants to use stereotypical female and male workers in order to attract customers to its stores. Sandra's rattail and unconventional gender presentation break with compulsory heteronormativity and perhaps even make some customers uncomfortable. The Walmart manager understood that Sandra's look was a risk for his local store and mandated that she change it. Mauricio and Laura were also disciplined for violating the company's idea of a standardized image.

In addition to abuse by managers over their personhood, retail workers at Walmart Chile have also been subjected to a serious and growing amount of violence from customers (Paulina Rubio, worker, interview 2012). In interviews I had with workers and worker leaders the issue of customer abuse consistently came up. Marcela, a cashier, said, "they [customers] always yell at us and blame us for the long lines, but we don't make those decisions" (interview 2012). Tania, another cashier says, "they [customers] have a temper tantrum and we have no recourse, we can't protect ourselves. We can't yell back. We just have to smile and be pleasant, while our selfhood is being attacked" (interview 2012). Both of these examples point to the emotional labor (Hochschild 1983) involved in the service economy. As McDowell astutely points out, "the physical production of a particular appearance and the deferential performance of an often-scripted exchange are an essential part of embodied social relations and the construction of identity in the workplace" (2009, 191). Workers at the frontlines of customer service, especially cashiers, bear the brunt of customer abuse, managing customers' emotions, while being appropriately feminine, servile, and professional. Abuse by customers toward workers in Chile has an additional layer of complexity, especially at Híper Líder, where there are significant differences in social class. Although much of the abuse endured by Walmart retail workers can be attributed to the classism that is prevalent in Chilean society (Méndez 2008; Stillerman 2010), an additional layer of classism specifically relates to the employer/domestic dynamic. A number of women I interviewed, who had previously been domestic workers, felt that some of the working conditions they had experienced as domestic workers prevailed in the customer/worker relationship in the stores. Specifically, workers reported that they felt like some upper-middle class clients treated them as though they were the "help" in their households.[2] The same status and power dynamics that are played inside private homes with domestic workers are played out publically on the retail floor. Casanova (2013, 572) points out that,

---

2. The seven former domestic workers I interviewed reported that when they worked as domestic workers they would be given some cash to make daily purchases at the grocery store or farmers market, but that the families generally made household purchases for the week, not trusting domestic workers with credit cards and significant sums of money.

"bodies are seen as carrying different amounts of social worth." This idea is applicable to what happens at Walmart Chile. The institution (Walmart) values wealthy Chileans over its workers, and wealthy Chileans see themselves as carrying more social worth than the working class women who work in the stores (or in their homes). In one typical situation, a wealthy woman called over a retail worker, barking, "Hey, girl, [snapping fingers] get me that can of preserved king crab." I saw this dynamic time and time again on the retail floor.

Globally, customer violence seems to be on the upswing. Wolkowitz argues, "customer abuse faced by workers arises partly from the way the job is organized, but also that abuse is exacerbated by cost-cutting measures that make abuse from the customer more likely" (2006, 109). Walmart places special emphasis on "service to customers" (Walmart 2011). This emphasis on customer service places a significant burden on workers who most directly deal with customers (cashiers, butchers, fishmongers, customer service, and restockers). These workers are more likely to have to do significant amounts of emotional labor on a daily basis as angry customers complain about not finding merchandise, returning merchandise, or long lines. Walmart could ease customer frustration, for example by opening up more cashier stations when lines are long, but having to hire more workers could cut into their profits. According to union leaders, Walmart Chile makes careful calculations about what kinds of lines customers are willing to tolerate. Cashiers then are at the front lines of managing customer emotions and acting as a shield for bad company practices.

Wages, Hours, and Breaks

Walmart is well known for pushing the boundaries of the law when it comes to wages, hours, and breaks. Because these things happen at the individual level, Walmart is sometimes successful in cheating retail workers out of pay and breaks.

On May 21, 2011, the president of the Federación Autónoma Walmart got a call from a worker who had a traumatic experience and was reaching out for help. Rosana, a cashier at Acuenta, asked her manager if she could take a break to use the bathroom. He said, "no." She told him that using the bathroom was her fundamental right. He said, "no." Desperate, she left her post and went to the bathroom. While she was using the facilities, her boss began screaming at her through the door. Then she heard a click. He had locked her inside the bathroom. She pounded on the door and screamed for someone to let her out. According to Sandra, the union leader I interviewed, Rosana's boss said, "this should teach you a lesson about who is in charge." He kept her in the bathroom for over two hours before sending her home. Rosana was granted paid medical leave for several weeks as a result of the trauma. What's striking is that Rosana's story is not uncommon. Countless workers I talked to complained that they often experienced difficulties getting permission to use the restroom, especially during peak shopping seasons. Workers also told me stories of cashiers having to wear diapers during peak seasons such as Christmas and Chilean independence day. I have no direct evidence of such cases. Once again, we can link these examples to managerial control over bodies and in general infantilizing workers. In this case it isn't about controlling the way a particular worker looks, but rather using a worker's body as a tool for domination. If a worker "misbehaves," the punishment is not letting them use the bathroom, locking them inside a bathroom, or putting them in a position where they must wear diapers.

Like Walmart workers in the United States, Chilean workers often complained that wages at Walmart were too low and that they could barely make ends meet. Carmen, makes and interesting observation, "I work and work and work, but no matter how much I work, I still don't earn enough money to shop here without going into debt. How is this possible?" (interview 2011). However, unlike unionized workers at U.S. supermarkets such as Ralphs, Kroger, and Fairway, who earn considerably more money and have better benefits than Walmart workers, Chilean workers in unions across the industry, with the exception of department store workers, earn very low wages. In fact, Walmart retail workers earn more than most other supermarket workers, yet they earn only about US$341 per month.[3] This income is simply not enough to live on. A 360-square foot one-bedroom apartment in a lower middle-class neighborhood costs about US$324 per month. Housing costs alone are only slightly below the average Walmart monthly wage. Walmart workers have to commute

---

3. This number is as of January 11, 2016.The minimum wage goes up every year in Chile.

significant distances to come to work or live with their parents if they are unmarried or students.

Furthermore, because of Chile's neoliberal economic transformation, employers are not paying into a pension plan, 401(k), or any other kind of retirement system for any workers in Chile. Workers are forced to participate in a retirement system that functions as a savings account. Because Chile has no social security system, Walmart retail and warehouse workers are unlikely to be able to retire. Employers are also not responsible for paying for health insurance. Workers must have health insurance in order to work, but the employer does not pay for it.

Another chief complaint that workers had was about getting enough hours. This complaint is consistent with other studies of the retail industry (Campusano 2015; Urrutia 2015). A permanent, full-time position at Walmart in Chile requires a forty-five-hour week. However, many workers, perhaps even a majority of retail workers, at Walmart Chile are working only twenty to thirty hours per week. These part-time jobs mean not only less money but also that such employees miss out on some of the benefits that full-time, permanent workers receive. Most part-time workers I interviewed wanted to be working full-time, but they were simply not given this opportunity. Furthermore, according to workers, store managers often used hours and schedules as a way of rewarding their favorite employees and punishing those who were making "trouble." Isabel says, "I was about to be promoted to a full-time worker, but then it fell through. So I started talking to the union. As soon as they [managers] saw me as a troublemaker, they changed my shift and reduced my hours" (interview 2014). As in the United States, Walmart in Chile relies on precarious labor to boost its significant profits, which were US$1 billion in 2014 (Walmart 2014). These profits may not sound excessive in comparison to the US$21 billion that Walmart made in the United States in 2014, but Chile is a country of 17,000,000 people, whereas the United States counts nearly 320,000,000. Furthermore, Chile generated a quarter of Walmart's international profit (i.e., gross profit).

Antiunion Practices

Much as in the United States, Walmart in Chile is at the forefront of antiunion practices. Such activity is slightly more challenging in Chile, because it cannot legally eliminate unions, but the company certainly tries its best to push the boundaries of what is legal and what it might be able to get away with.

Union Meetings   Under Chilean labor law, union members have the right to hold meetings in their workplace. In January 2011, Walmart announced that it would no longer allow union members to meet inside the stores during their lunch hour, blatantly breaking the law. According to Sandra, the company gave the justification that if it allowed unions to have meetings in the store, it would have to allow the same opportunity to all worker organizations, including for example the company soccer team. Workers and their unions perceived the decision as an excuse to not allow unions to run their daily affairs on the shop floor.

The announcement that unions would no longer be able to meet during lunch hour in stores was a particularly hard blow for the autonomous unions, which have few resources. Meetings are especially challenging for women who often have childcare obligations before and after work. Their dues compensation is so low, especially because it is collected on an individual store level, that they cannot pay for office space. Autonomous unions need the physical space of the supermarket to hold meetings, draft grievances, and have the opportunity to talk to workers on a daily basis.

Benefits in Exchange for Union Representation   In 2009, as the autonomous unions were just starting to organize themselves, Walmart attempted a number of legal tactics to obstruct them. When these attempts failed, it shifted to a union-busting tactic that is well known in the United States. It started reaching out to groups of workers it did not want involved in strikes, including department managers and other workers in leadership positions. Walmart offered them higher wages, a productivity bonus, and two other bonuses in exchange for them agreeing not to bargain collectively with the union—in other words, a better deal, at least in the short term, than a collective bargaining agreement. This union-busting strategy is common in Chile (Durán and Kremerman 2015; Urrutia 2015). Of course, no retail worker in a leadership position would join a union whose collective bargaining agreement would not cover her. The courts sanctioned Walmart for its antiunion practices, which are a labor law violation (Court of Appeals San Miguel 2011; González Santibáñez 2012). Unfortunately, this written sanction with a minor fine did not prevent Walmart from attempting the strategy again.

In 2010, during collective bargaining negotiations for stores in Valdivia (southern Chile), Walmart once again offered a differential benefits package. This time Walmart argued that it was not engaged in antiunion practices because workers in middle management and other leadership positions in stores could choose between the collective bargaining agreement or the "benefits package." The union filed with the courts and the judge quickly understood that Walmart was trying to keep middle managers out of the union. It is important to note that the previously filed legal brief with the court in Santiago had established precedent, and the judge in this case was able to not only sanction Walmart for antiunion practices but also to force the company to allow all employees who signed up for the benefits package an opportunity to bargain collectively at any time (González Santibáñez 2012; Valdivia Court 2010).

Ekono Strike   In March 2011, Ekono workers went on strike. It was the first strike by workers who were attempting to unionize under Walmart proper. Walmart understood that Chile was watching, and it was accordingly strategic in its approach to the strike. It did not fire participants, nor was it heavy handed in any other way. Still, Walmart engaged in a number of antiunion practices, one for which it was sanctioned and forced to pay back wages.

Workers in Chile are generally paid on a monthly basis, but Ekono paid its employees biweekly, in order to give workers some breathing space in the middle of the month, since their wages are so low. This practice of paying on a biweekly basis was written into the labor contract that each employee had to sign. Workers went on strike on March 11, but Walmart did not pay the striking workers their due from having worked the first ten days of the month. Withholding payment not only violated the labor contract, but the courts also considered it to be an antiunion practice; only those workers who went on strike were targeted, thus hurting the union. It was also injurious to the union because it prevented other workers from joining the strike for fear of losing their meager wages, which further eroded the union's collective bargaining strength (González Santibáñez 2012). Walmart was forced to pay over US$50,000 in back wages to around 300 workers, but not until long after the strike had ended.

In the aftermath of the strike, Walmart also engaged in other types of antiunion behavior that are more difficult to prove. Union leaders claim that Walmart shifted the strike's leaders into different stores to defuse their power in their home stores. The company also started harassing leaders of the strike and forcing them to take drug tests, which were not universally imposed. Alejandro, the president of the Ekono union says "I've never once been drug tested, and now all of the sudden [after the strike] they want to test us? I mean, it's absurd (interview 2011). Both of these actions are illegal but very difficult to prove. According to union leaders at Ekono, Walmart claims that it shifts workers to different stores frequently based on having the right balance of expertise in different locations. But as Esteban, one of the union leaders states, "it's true that workers are sometimes moved to different stores, but are you really going to tell me that they didn't move us because of the strike? We are not fools. It's not coincidence that the leaders of the strike were moved" (interview 2011).

Three times a year the Chilean Ministry of Labor announces the top companies who have engaged in antiunion behavior. They are fined and not allowed to participate in government contracts for at least two years. In 2012 the leading retailers who were sanctioned for their continuous antiunion practices were Walmart and Starbucks (Dirección de Trabajo 2012). In fact, Walmart was sanctioned for these practices in 2009 (its first year in Chile), 2011, 2012, 2015, and 2016. Antiunion practices included firing workers who were protected by the union, noncompliance with union contracts, and interfering with the process of unionization (Dirección del Trabajo 2009, 2011, 2012b, 2015, 2016). Companies on the state's list are generally fined between US$50,000 and US$100,000. Although these fines do not seriously impact Walmart's profit margins, they do hurt the company's reputation, which could impact profit margins down the road.

These bad working conditions, human rights violations, antiunion practices, and other violations of the law may not be surprising to U.S. readers, who are used to hearing about Walmart's egregious practices. Nonetheless, these examples are significant in Chile, not because they do not occur in other companies, but because they are deemed important enough to be sanctioned, even by a weak labor law system.

Union Democracy, Organizing Tactics, and Strategic Capacity

Chilean retail workers are fighting the variety of abuses at Walmart and making significant gains in the process. To fight Goliath, Walmart workers employ a model of flexible militancy (to recap, strategic capacity, militancy, and union democracy), strengthened by their autonomy from mainstream labor organizations such as the Central Unitaria de Trabajadores.

Strikes and Strike Threats   The most important factor in retail workers' strategy is their ability to disrupt Walmart's operations. In the Ekono strike on March 11, 2011, over 300 workers at over twenty stores in Santiago walked off the job. They were the first store format to have formed a union under Walmart proper in August 2010. Ten workers started to organize the union in early 2010. They were fed up with low wages and poor working conditions, especially because Walmart workers in the other format stores were making more money and had better working conditions than they did. Esteban, one of the leaders of the union and strike said, "because the Ekono stores are so small, we were responsible for doing everything at the store from heating up bread, to sweeping floors, cashiering, and stocking shelves. Yet, they didn't want to pay us for all this expertise" (Estaban, interview 2011). Several of these union leaders, who were mostly young men, had gained some union experience from other workplaces. For example, some had worked in agriculture and others in movie theaters. They had a clear understanding that the conditions for Ekono workers would not improve without a union. Furthermore, all of the Ekono stores (about sixty across Chile) operated under one tax identification number and could therefore form a single union. Worker activists seized this opportunity to create one union that would represent nearly 1,000 workers.

In March 2011, Ekono workers were negotiating their first collective bargaining agreement. Their main demand was a 10 percent wage increase, to be retroactively applied over two years. Walmart representatives did not show up at three bargaining sessions (Esteban, interview, 2011). When its representatives finally did sit at the table, they offered a 0.05 percent wage increase over the next four years, amounting to about US$1.50 per month. Infuriated and frustrated with this offer, workers took to the streets. The strike lasted one month during which they protested Walmart's low wages, poor benefits, and bad working conditions, including forcing workers to return to work before the end of lunch breaks (Esteban, interview 2011; Schnitzer 2011). Alexis, the secretary of the union, states,

We have the worst working conditions imaginable. For example, we get attendance bonuses, right, and those bonuses are for perfect attendance. So if you miss a day of work because you are sick, you lose wages for the day and you lose the attendance bonus for the month. You [as a worker] are conditioned to work all the time. And even if you have a workplace accident and you are given permission by the insurance company to miss work because of the injury, you still lose the bonus. And we are constantly harassed and intimidated by managers. They constantly threaten to file disciplinary charges against us for ridiculous things. For example, they will write you up for working extra hours without requesting it in writing first, but they will also write you up for leaving on time and not completing your work. Workers can't win under this system. (interview 2011)

Workers protested in front of many of the Ekono stores across Santiago and raised consumer awareness about Walmart's bad labor practices. "It was a difficult strike to maintain, because Ekono workers are spread across Santiago, and there are very few workers in each store, and as a new union we have essentially no resources" (Esteban, interview, 2011). Through the Consejo de Trabajadores Walmart Chile, the Ekono workers received significant support from the two main Walmart retail federations at the time, as well as their affiliate unions. They also received legal advice and advocacy from two of the part-time lawyers working for unions in the Consejo.

Ultimately, the contract negotiations were settled with a US$1.50 monthly increase, the original offer that Walmart made, but the strike was important for building organization. Furthermore, the strike gave workers enough leverage to not have to accept a four-year contract but rather agree to re-opening contract negotiations in eighteen months (Esteban, interview, 2011). The three Ekono union leaders I interviewed all agreed that the strike taught them valuable lessons about organizing, mobilizing, and solidarity. Even though they were frustrated that workers did not want to stay on strike for more than a month, they felt better prepared to lead their union. In the months after the strike union leaders spent a significant amount of time building the infrastructure of their union. They set up committees, tried to reach workers at all Ekono stores in Santiago, and started having membership meetings. The Ekono union leadership was also at the forefront of challenging the system whereby Walmart hires fewer workers and expects them to work in many different capacities (see Chapter 3). Walmart's job description for Ekono workers gives us some insights into the company's expectations:

> Must help customers with their purchases in an efficient, courteous, friendly and respectful way; operate cash register and perform cashier duties; security; restock; bake bread; and execute all related tasks. . . . Qualifications: a) high school diploma b) very flexible, honest, and have a high energy level c) experience in small store or convenience store preferred d) no experience in supermarkets. (Negociación Colectiva Ekono 2012)

Unlike in the other format stores, polyfunctionality is built into the job description at Ekono. Polyfunctionality is not illegal in Chile; however, the law is quite specific about the ways it can be used. The intent of the law is for an employer to be able to specify a couple of related tasks in the labor contract. Walmart has been trying to exceed the limits of the law by making Ekono workers perform *all* jobs. The union has been working with several legal advisers to challenge these issues in the courts, especially since Walmart continues to reduce the number of workers at each Ekono store, constituting a speed-up, or forcing workers to do more work for the same amount of money. In addition to testing the limits at Ekono, Walmart has also tried to implement certain aspects of polyfunctionality at other format stores with limited success.

The other local unions affiliated with the Federación Autónoma and FENATRALID also threatened strikes during 2012, 2013, and 2015 contract negotiations. In all cases, strikes were averted due to militant action by leaders and members leading up to contract negotiations. Ekono workers also threatened another strike in their reopened negotiations in 2012. Willingness to organize and participate in militant action leading up to contract negotiations can be transformative and contribute to building power even when, as in the first Ekono strike, they do not result in significant economic gains.

Legal Strategy: Fundamental Rights Walmart retail workers have had incredible success using innovative legal tactics that form part of their strategic capacity to fight on issues of fundamental rights and antiunion behavior. Union members, leaders, and lawyers meet on a regular basis to devise the legal strategy. Members are trained in labor law and participate in union leadership academies, leaders find labor law violations in the retail stores, and the two part-time lawyers put the cases together.

When Sandra was disciplined and nearly fired for having a rattail and Mauricio for having a beard, the union could have called a strike, picketing, or other kind of job action, but instead leaders decided to educate coworkers about rights at work, while at the same time shaming the manager of the store where the incidents took place by marching silently with signs throughout the store. The "Rights at Work" campaign served two important purposes. First, it was a great opportunity to provide workers with political education. Second, by mobilizing workers and community members to force the company into concessions by using their moral authority to publically shame the company, the union effectively used symbolic leverage. As a result of the organizing and the march there was an outpouring of support to file a legal case with the department of labor, and significant activity and discussion in retail stores where workers had suffered similar indignities.

Walmart headquarters was taken aback by the angry workers. They settled out of court with the union, which asked them to publically apologize to the two workers and publish that apology in the company newsletter for two weeks. The apology read:

> We publically apologize to Sandra and Mauricio for having received treatment from an ex-employee [the manager] that is not compatible with the dignity that every worker deserves and is not compatible with the values and culture of our company. Walmart has already taken the necessary steps to ensure that the same situation does not repeat itself. We ask that Sandra and Mauricio accept our public apology. Once again, we want to reiterate that what took place does not represent the ideas or actions of the company in terms of the fundamental rights of workers. It has never been the intention of the Supermercado Líder (Walmart) to damage the honor of one of our employees (Hípermercado Líder Matucana, 2011).

This acknowledgment was a significant victory for Walmart workers. The letter shows the deep contradictions in the company. On the one hand, it states that the manager's behavior was "not compatible with the values and culture of our company"; on the other hand, the manager was only abiding by what had been made clear to him in the Walmart handbook.

Even apart from what was written in the handbook, the manager understood that a certain aesthetic attracted customers. By publically apologizing and publishing the letter, Walmart had to clarify that it could in fact not discriminate based on appearances.

This victory is a great example of successfully leveraging symbolic power and the significant agency that workers have in their workplaces, especially when they are organized and represented by a militant union. Furthermore, this victory, particularly the public apology that thousands of workers saw, mobilized others to fight against Walmart's attacks on their fundamental rights and stand up for respect on the job. Subsequent lawsuits were filed around issues of dress, grooming, and body appearance, such as piercings and tattoos.

Another significant legal victory involved the expansion of Walmart culture in Chile. It is well established in the sociology of work that shifting the language from "worker" or "employee" to "associate" or "team member" is an important managerial tactic for hegemonic control. The term "worker" can lead to class-consciousness, which employers, especially Walmart, would like to avoid. At the heart of the corporation's culture is to call workers "associates." In the United States, the term "associate" is used to build a sense of ownership or participation in a family. Walmart associates are also shareholders. For years this approach had much success in the United States, but since 2012 the low pay and poor working conditions at Walmart along with the formation of the Organization United for Respect at Walmart (OUR Walmart) has weakened some of the power of Walmart culture. For example, since 2012 OUR Walmart has been organizing Black Friday strikes. In Los Angeles, the Pico Rivera Walmart, which was at the center of labor organizing activity and had significant strike participation, closed temporarily in April 2015. Four other stores in other states also closed. Each of these stores had significant strike participation. OUR Walmart workers claim that stores closed due to labor activity. Walmart claimed plumbing problems. After significant pressure from community, labor, and religious groups, the Pico Rivera store reopened in September 2015 (Masunaga 2015). For the most part, Walmart has nonetheless been successful in maintaining and fostering "Walmart Culture." In Chile this has been more difficult for the company.

About a year after Walmart entered Chile it introduced the concept of Walmart culture. The independent unions I was working with at the time were rather dubious. One of the first aspects of the culture that Walmart tried to introduce was calling workers "associates." This concept was not entirely new in Chile, since D&S would sometimes call workers *colaboradores* or *asociados*. For D&S the practice was informal and not officially written in any contracts or legal employment documents; it was not central to managerial culture. However, Walmart pushed the concept heavily and incorporated it into official documents. Its push for workers to widely adopt the language of colaborador backfired, in part because some workers who had been radicalized through their union activism connected the concept to the term "collaborator," defined by Merriam-Webster as "to cooperate with or willingly assist an enemy of one's country and especially an occupying force." It was an especially interesting word choice, since Walmart had other options. For example, in Mexico they use the term "asociado," which much more closely resembles "associate."

Needless to say, the independent unions Chile were outraged that their workers were being called "colaboradores," and in 2010, working in a united fashion, they filed a complaint with the ministry of labor objecting to the term and citing that the use of "colaboradores" is a violation of the labor code. Union leaders told me that they were ridiculed by the Sindicato Interempresa Líder (SIL) union for "making such a big deal" out of the word. However, the independent unions very clearly understood the implications this language had for Walmart culture. In January 2012, the ministry of labor ruled that calling workers "colaboradores" was indeed a violation of the labor code. The Santiago Norte Inspección Communal de Trabajo (Northern Santiago Regional Labor Inspectorate) stated,

> The term worker is a juridical concept, established explicitly in the law, article 3, section b of the labor code. If the legislator had wanted to make the term "worker" equivalent to the term "collaborator," he/she would have done so. As a result, the employer's interpretation is not applicable. In addition, the term places the employer and the employee in a seemingly horizontal relationship, without acknowledging the power relations that govern work and that create subordination and dependence on the employer. Therefore the company must modify its manual to reflect the language in the labor code. . . [T]he employer must make these corrections and/or changes within thirty business days of receipt of this document, understanding that it will be subject to administrative sanction if it does not abide with this ruling within the time period established. In addition, the employer must publicize

the changes as required by article 156 of the labor code.[4] (Inspección Communal de Trabajo, 2011; author translation)

This is one of the most significant symbolic victories that workers in Chile have had against Walmart. It defeated a principle that is critical to the way Walmart operates. It created a space for these unions to have a public dialogue with their members about why these terms are problematic. Walmart appealed the decision, but in the end the lower court's decision held. Worker activists have been using the ruling to fight against the term on a store level. Ricardo, states, "Every time I hear a manager say colaborador, I respond, 'you mean *trabajador*'? Every time they hand me a legal document that says colaborador, I make them rewrite it to say trabajador. That's how we wear them down" (Ricardo, interview, 2013).

Finally, many unions have spent time developing shop-steward structures and training members to watch out for potential shopfloor grievances. The new grievance strategy has yielded many new grievances with the Dirección de Trabajo. Of course, not all of these grievances have generated victories, and even when workers do win it doesn't mean that Walmart stops its unfair labor practices, but the grievance strategy does provide the opportunity for solidarity and union building. Furthermore, it has strengthened strategic capacity by bringing workers from the four formats together to collectively analyze issues that they are all facing and develop strategies for changing those problems across all the different store formats.

Direct Action   The two most common forms of direct action taken by the militant Walmart retail unions are street meetings and confrontations with management at both store and corporate levels.

In response to Walmart's unilateral declaration that unions could no longer have their lunchtime meetings inside stores, the various independent unions began to meet and have lunch in front of Híper Líder stores. These meetings continued throughout the month of May 2011 at different stores across Santiago. Workers and their supporters hung banners that read *Walmart Anti-Sindical* (Walmart is antiunion) and plugged an

---

4. Article 156 establishes that employees must be notified of the changes within thirty business days and that both unions and employees should receive, free of charge, a copy of the new company manual.

amplifier into an outlet inside the store to use a microphone and play loud music. They also passed out flyers to consumers as they conducted their union business. Walmart managers stood outside, writing down the names of workers who attended the meeting, but eventually they got tired of writing because greater numbers of workers kept coming out to attend the meeting. Managers tried unplugging the sound system multiple times, but workers just kept plugging it back in. At one of the meetings I attended workers voted in favor of a ten percent dues increase to rent their own space to have union meetings.

These street meetings were an especially good way of both publically shaming Walmart, while building a significant degree of worker solidarity and trust in one another. Walmart managers were visibly uncomfortable with the street meetings. Furthermore, the sizable protests disrupted customer service in the stores. While it was intimidating for many workers to take the leap and participate in a street meeting, as they saw their fellow co-workers join the meeting, they felt the strength in numbers. Karina said, "At first I was intimidated when I saw the managers watching [workers] outside of the store, but then I started seeing more and more people come out, and there was a lot of energy, so it moved me to also participate" (interview 2011). Most important, no workers were disciplined as a result of their participation in the street meeting, which gave them additional courage to become involved in the union.

Delegations to store-level managers and Walmart corporate offices have been an important source of union building and solidarity across unions. At the store level, these delegations have empowered worker members. For example, at the Líder Matucana, Alysia, says, "It is important for us to understand our power. When five of us [women] storm the manager's office it helps us to feel protected and give us strength. We use their own 'open-door policy' against them" (interview 2011). Carmen adds, "They think they can make us do whatever they want, but at this store we have job titles and we are going to enforce them" (Carmen, interview 2011). Carmen is referring to a store manager's attempt to make one of the women work as a stocker in the clothing department, because her job of weighing bread was slow. The women marched in and made clear that they were representing all of the workers in the store and would not do jobs that were not in their work contract. The manager backed off and sent the worker back to the bakery department.

On another occasion a Walmart manager was trying to interfere in a union election in a store where there was a fight between the independent union and the corrupt union. The leaders for the independent union reached out to the Consejo, and workers from the various Walmart unions marched on the store, picketed outside, and sent a delegation inside to tell the manager to butt out of the election. Ultimately, the manager agreed to comply if they would just stop picketing the store.

Coordinating across Locals   The militant retail unions I worked with acknowledged that in order to continue to grow and succeed they would need to begin to reach out to each other and collectively strategize. The incentives to do this are complicated, because Chilean labor law disincentivizes different unions from joining together (see chapter 2). It took a tremendous amount of trust to begin laying out the groundwork to create the Consejo de Trabajadores Walmart Chile. It was first attempted in 2010, and then again in 2011. Initially, the Consejo was limited to retail worker unions, but eventually these unions invited Logística, Transportación y Servicios because they recognized the strategic possibilities of an alliance between the warehouse and retail unions. The Consejo remains fragmented, but some of the unions continue to meet when they need support (see chapter 4). In 2013, they tried to negotiate collective bargaining agreements that would all expire on the same date. Although the unions pushed hard for this collective expiration date, Walmart was quick to understand the strategy and blocked it.

Outcomes

By 2012, the high level of worker organization at Ekono yielded extraordinary economic gains in the two-year contract. The new contract brought Ekono workers more on par with Líder and Híper Líder workers, though they still have a long way to go. The new contract included a 3.5 percent wage increase, a US$60 per month attendance bonus, a US$100 per month attendance bonus for night stockers,[5] a US$27 per month transportation

---

5. In the section of the collective bargaining agreement that refers to the attendance bonus, the union won language that stipulates that illness or workplace accidents cannot be used against a worker.

allowance, US$50 bonuses for Chilean independence day and Christmas, one summer and one winter uniform per year, a $US38 bonus for the birth of a child, a $US38 bonus for getting married and permission to not work on the wedding day, a US$400 death benefit for the spouse in case a worker passes away, and sixteen hours of release time per month for union leaders to conduct their union business (Negociación Colectiva Ekono 2012). These are dramatic changes from the 2011 contract. Before the union existed, Ekono workers were only guaranteed a minimum wage and benefits set forth by the labor code.

Contracts at the other independent unions in the retail industry have also included significant gains. In 2012, for the first time, independent unions were able to negotiate for wages and benefits above those set by the protection agreement signed between the SIL and Walmart. In the end, the general wage and benefits package was applied in similar form to all unionized Walmart workers (who were simultaneously bargaining), even members of the SIL, thanks to the flexible militancy of the independent unions, which created the strong associational power that led to effective disruption. In addition, the Federación Autónoma, which represents eight different local unions, five that bargained simultaneously in 2012, achieved an unprecedented bonus that was not applied to the other unionized workers. This bonus, paid only to members of the unions represented by the Federación, is given for years of service. It is paid monthly and is permanent. Full-time workers with less than two years of service get an additional US$35.75 per month, workers with more than five years but less than six years of service receive US$75.40 (see Table 5.1). This may not seem like much money by U.S. standards, but most retail workers earn a minimum wage of US$383 dollars per month, so a bonus of US$35 or US$75 per month is nearly a 10 percent or 20 percent wage increase, respectively. Subsequently, the FENATRALID was able to negotiate and win this benefit for its members in 2014 (Negociación Colectiva FENATRALID, 2014).

Furthermore, in the 2015 contract for the Federación Autónoma these seniority sums went up an additional 14 percent across the board. In addition, cashiers received increased bonuses for purchases paid for with the Presto credit card, or if customers paid their credit card bill at the register. The union also negotiated a bonus for occasional night-shift workers. They negotiated for better food in the cafeteria and additional uniforms for work. Furthermore, the Federación Autónoma negotiated 100 hours

TABLE 5.1. Bonuses based on seniority, 2013

Seniority by year in enterprise	Gross value
1 year and less than 2	Pesos/Dollars
18 hours	7.200/14.18
30 hours	12.060/23.76
45 hours	18.000/35.47
2 years and less than 3	
18 hours	9.200/18.12
30 hours	15.410/30.36
45 hours	23.000/45.31
3 years and less than 4	
18 hours	11.200/22.06
30 hours	18.760/37.00
45 hours	28.000/55.16
4 years and less than 5	
18 hours	12.800/25.22
30 hours	21.440/42.24
45 hours	32.000/63.04
5 years and less than 6	
18 hours	15.200/30.00
30 hours	25.460/50.16
45 hours	38.000/74.86

Source: Negociación Colectiva Federación Autónoma 2012.

per month of release time for union work for members of the executive committees of each of its affiliate unions and 350 hours per month for the executive committee of the federation itself. This is an unprecedented amount of release time to engage in the daily life of the union. Finally, one of the most important topics negotiated was work schedules. Previously, work schedules were determined exclusively by the needs of management. However, the 2015 contract stipulates that if a worker is scheduled for the morning, midday, or evening shift, they must have the same schedule for their entire workweek. Furthermore, workers must receive their monthly schedule no later than the twenty-fifth of each month (Negociación Colectiva Federación Autónoma, 2015).

As a result of the street meetings that were held across Santiago, Walmart reversed its decision and told the unions that they could continue meeting inside the stores. Some of the independent unions, however, rejected the offer. Sandra states, "We realized that we were dependent on the company to conduct union business, which is our right as union members. We don't want to be dependent; we have decided to find space outside of the store to meet" (Sandra, interview, 2011). Nonetheless this is an important victory for workers who want to meet in the store.

Members of the militant and autonomous retail federations also made impressive gains in terms of dignity and respect in the workplace. Their model of flexible militancy allows them to respond to workplace concerns as they come up on the shop floor. By consistently demonstrating their militancy, Walmart retail workers have created a culture of nonconformity. On a monthly basis, these workers are participating in delegations to management, protesting in the streets, and submitting legal charges. Even when they are not specifically challenging management, they are demonstrating their strength on the shop floor. For example, for Mother's Day 2016, Sandra Neida decided that she would hire a Mariachi band to celebrate working mothers in the store. Without special permission from Walmart, she walked into the store with the Mariachi band in tow and paraded around celebrating mothers. Managers were visibly uncomfortable with the disruption; yet they said absolutely nothing. This anecdote gives some sense of the strong union culture inside some of Walmart's retail stores.

In 2015 the Federación held a successful strike authorization vote. Such tactics have management on notice. As a result of this militancy and the flexibility with which they respond to workplace injustices, these federations have leveraged their symbolic power to challenge the heart of Walmart's antiworker practices: Walmart culture. Although they haven't been able to achieve the same economic gains as the warehouse workers, they have won significant victories in terms of rights and respect at work. All of the autonomous retail federations have participated in ensuring these outcomes, but the Federación Autónoma really shines in terms of its strategic capacity and union democracy. It has been able to create a path forward for itself and the other retail unions.

During the 2012 and 2013 contract negotiations one of the collective decisions that the unions participating in the Consejo took was to try to coordinate contract expiration dates. These unions recognized that they could significantly improve their social power if their contracts expired at the same time and they all coordinated a strike action together. Of course, it is difficult to coordinate contract expiration dates because management understands this strategy very well and is not interested in negotiating on this issue. In this particular case, Walmart spread misinformation among the different unions, creating a sense of mistrust among the organizations. Because these groups have not yet established significant trust among each other, it proved difficult to counter Walmart's strategy of divide and rule. Unfortunately, the unions were not successful in coordinating contract expiration dates. They would have probably needed to go on strike over this issue, and the unions and their members were not yet prepared to do so. Ultimately, these unions will need to find a way to build a more trusting relationship to strengthen their leverage against Walmart.

Conclusion

In its retail operations in Chile, Walmart has been true to its reputation. The company has engaged in its characteristic antiunion behavior. It has created low-wage, precarious jobs with little opportunity for mobility. Workers have suffered from customer abuse, polyfunctionality, and violations of fundamental and human rights. Nonetheless, Chilean Walmart workers have shown the capacity to stand up against this transnational against the odds and make significant progress on achieving better working conditions. However, not all Chilean Walmart workers have been as successful as the ones in this chapter. Workers who are members of autonomous unions that combine militant and democratic unionism have fared much better than other Walmart workers. This can be easily observed in the retail stores themselves. I spent many months visiting Walmart stores across Santiago, and it was clear when I was walking into a store that had a strong union leadership versus a store that had either no union or a weak union. Workers at the weakly organized stores did not have the same level of confidence. They routinely asked managers for permission to take breaks or go to the bathroom. They were also more likely to accept authority and hierarchical decision making. It was evident in these stores that workers did not feel ownership over their work lives or their union. On the other hand, workers in stores with a militant union leadership displayed self-confidence. For example, they simply stated that they were going on breaks or to the bathroom, they did not ask for permission. If there was a problem, they routinely sought out the shop steward or told managers that they were going to talk to the union. These workers also were more likely to confront management about calling them traba-jadores and not colaboradores. Finally, workers in highly organized stores understood their rights and understood that they could contest manage-ment decisions that they saw as unfair.

6

LOOKING BACK AND GOING FORWARD

The story of Walmart in Chile provides a counternarrative to most books and articles about the company. The authors of the expansive literature on Walmart generally fall into two camps—those who embrace the company's strategy and mission, and those who critique the company's unscrupulous practices. However, little has been written about how workers challenge Walmart. This lack of research is not unusual, as there has been little success organizing Walmart in the United States. Furthermore, what has been written on worker organizing generally describes Walmart's international operations (Bank Muñoz et al. forthcoming). Some scholars have suggested that maybe Walmart is not as terrible in Chile as it is in the United States; however, my interviews and firsthand observations show that many of Walmart's bad labor practices are similar to those used in the United States. Walmart pays slightly higher wages in comparison to the rest of the supermarket industry in Chile; nonetheless, it is constantly pushing the limits of Chilean labor law. Still, Chilean Walmart workers have been able to achieve better pay and working conditions by building up their capacity for disruption. As Piven and Cloward (1978) and Jenkins (2002) have astutely pointed out, it is this capacity for disruption that forces the employer's hand. Retail workers have been most successful in employing symbolic disruption (public shaming, disrupting services, and making their issues a moral cause), while warehouse workers have successfully leveraged their structural power, first by forcing D&S's hand in a 2006 strike by disrupting production, and later by waging effective strike threats against Walmart proper. In order to have the capacity for disruption, Chile's Walmart unions needed to build strong associational power, the power that comes from the collective organization of workers (Wright 2000). In addition, the warehouse union benefitted by leveraging its structural power, the power that comes from its strategic location in the system (Wright 2000). Walmart Chile's retail and warehouse unions have built strong associational power by creating unions with high levels of strategic capacity, militancy, and union democracy. However, given different political histories, and varied associational and structural power, these unions have established different models of unionism.

Retail workers, who comprise the majority of Walmart's nearly 40,000 employees in Chile, are scattered across Santiago, not to mention the length of Chile, and have less overall structural power than warehouse workers, who are concentrated in three warehouses in Santiago and can shut down the supply chain if they go on strike. As the public face of Walmart, retail workers have more symbolic leverage, or the power of shaming, public drama, and moral authority (Chun 2009), than warehouse workers do, and they have used this symbolic leverage to extract economic and noneconomic victories at the bargaining table.

The warehouse union Logística, Transportación y Servicios (LTS) is best represented by what I call "strategic democracy," whereas the retail workers' unions are best characterized by "flexible militancy" (for more on these two concepts, see chapter 3). Strategic democracy highlights a strong democratic tradition, a high level of political education and leadership development, and strategic capacity. Unlike other Chilean warehouse unions, the LTS union has effectively leveraged its structural power, not only in times of contract negotiations, but in a consistent way, even in between contract expirations. It has successfully leveraged its structural power by building a union where members have significant decision-making power and take ownership over the day-to-day operations of the organization.

The vibrant shopfloor culture is in part of a result of a union structure in which all members have to participate in the *escuela sindical* (union school), where members learn about the basics of unionism, such as how to organize, understanding budgets, and the role of shopfloor stewards, and, more importantly, receive political education, including labor history, working-class history, and political theory (Marx, Gramsci, Smith). One of the most important things they learn in the escuela sindical is mapping production, which comes from Gramsci's idea that worker councils inside the factory would give workers the power to control production. Chilean warehouse workers map production by controlling information about the flow of goods into and out of the warehouse. Mapping production has significantly increased workers' capacity for disruption, because it gives them real-time knowledge that allows them to make quick strategic decisions. For example, the systematic process of mapping production allows them to decide what pallets are most strategic to either hold back or release to retail stores. Mapping production has also been an effective organizing tool because it helps build horizontal networks and knowledge, requiring the widespread participation of the membership. As a result, building a democratic union with high levels of membership participation has allowed LTS to enhance its strategic capacity. LTS members have also benefitted from their initial high levels of militancy during the strike. At the union's inception this militancy, helped shape the perception of management that it was much stronger than it originally was, and offered members the time and space to build a much more powerful union. Since its first strike in 2006, LTS has been able to extract gains at the bargaining table by simply threatening to strike, and most of the time it has not needed to do even that.

Furthermore, being autonomous from political parties and the Central Unitaria de Trabajadores (CUT), the mainstream national labor federation, gives the union the flexibility and creativity to pursue its own agenda. In the end, LTS's model has allowed it to make unprecedented economic gains. In addition, it has been creative in its contract negotiations, allowing it to negotiate a collective productivity bonus, rather than an individual one. This was a huge victory, because it allowed the union to further its efforts of creating a workplace consciousness that promotes the collective over the individual.

Walmart retail workers, by contrast, have had to confront other challenges in the industry and workplace. Retail worker activists have different political histories and experiences from warehouse workers. Their model of unionism—flexible militancy—is also characterized by strategic capacity and union democracy, but these unions have developed such characteristics differently. Since 2011 the retail unions have been more consistently militant than the warehouse union. Furthermore, because they are spread out across Santiago, these workers have had to develop an ability to be flexible and more responsive to conditions in individual retail stores. Their strengths have been in direct-action tactics, delegations to the boss, and a creative legal strategy. The legal strategy is especially consistent with some of the findings in Crocco and Crocco's (2015) work on unions and legal strategy.

The retail unions I worked with, particularly those that are members of the two labor federations, Federación Autónoma and FENATRALID, care deeply about union democracy, but because of how spread out they are and their different political legacies, they have been less successful in attaining the same kind of membership participation and grassroots decision making as the warehouse union. These two retail federations also have a number of differences in their cultures. For example, FENATRALID is a slightly older, more experienced federation. Natalia Duque, the president of the federation has significant experience both as a worker and as a leader and is finishing up her college education. She is also one of the few leaders who had prior experience with the labor movement. Natalia's federation also represents many cashiers, who have more structural power within the retail industry than other workers. Conversely, Sandra Neida, president of the Federación Autónoma is more of a firebrand. She is new to the labor movement, but has clear ideals and goals for the movement. Perhaps the unions that have come closest to developing the same kinds of democratic structures as LTS are members of the Federación Autónoma, which in 2014 started developing more political education for its members. The retail unions have been most successful in leveraging symbolic disruption, which has been particularly effective in resolving issues of fundamental and human rights, but these workers have also made concrete, if modest, economic gains.

The case studies of Walmart workers in Chile illustrate that despite challenges in Chile's institutional and regulatory climate, particularly labor law reform, Walmart workers have been making substantive improvements to their workplace lives through their unions' commitment to building power from below. Three themes emerge from this story: first, Walmart is organizable; second, institutional and regulatory context matter; third, building power from below is key.

Walmart Is Organizable

In the 1980s many U.S.-based unionists and labor scholars argued that immigrants, particularly low-wage Latino/as, were not organizable. For some, they were not organizable because of their tenuous immigration status (many were undocumented), for others they were not organizable because industry was shifting off shore. Yet others believed that immigrants were simply too fearful. This argument was not new, as the same was said for young women working in the garment industry at the beginning of the twentieth century. New York City's garment workers not only organized, they also were responsible for the passage of sweeping labor rights legislation in the 1920s and 1930s (Greenwald 2005). Seventy years later immigrant workers in southern California revitalized a failing labor movement (Milkman 2000). Walmart workers in Chile are continuing this legacy. Living in the United States, it is hard to believe that Walmart workers can win, given the corporation's merciless attacks on workers and their unions throughout the supply chain. Yet across the globe Walmart workers have successfully organized. Walmart workers are unionized not only in Chile, but also in Argentina, Brazil, Mexico, Central America, South Africa, the United Kingdom, and China (Chan 2011). Not all of these unions are as effective or democratic as the Chilean unions in this book. Nonetheless, globally, Walmart has been forced to reckon with unions. In Chile, it has had to not only withstand unionization but also produce good collective bargaining agreements.

If Walmart is unionized around the globe, why not the United States? A number of factors make organizing Walmart workers in the United States particularly challenging. First, U.S. labor law is weak. Employers have much more power to defeat unions in the United States than in many other parts of the world. For example, the bar for organizing a union is quite high. U.S. unions need 30 percent of the bargaining unit to sign membership cards before they can ask for a National Labor Relations Board (NLRB) election (NLRB 2016). In reality, if the union has any chance of winning the election, it must collect a strong majority of signatures before the election. In Chile, the bar for unionization is set low; workers are allowed to form a union (which the employer must recognize) without prior authorization and without an election. To engage in collective bargaining 30 percent of workers in the bargaining unit must be members of the union (Dirección del Trabajo 2012a). In addition to the advantage of a high bar for unionization, U.S. employers can replace striking workers, lock out workers, and otherwise campaign against unions with little consequence. In Chile, employers also have the right to replace striking workers and lock out workers, but it was limited in scope during the formation of the unions in this book.

Second, Walmart has waged serious antiunion campaigns in the United States. It has spent millions of dollars on antiunion consultants and antiunion training programs for its managers. This spending is in sharp contrast to Walmart in other countries, where the corporation was forced to accept preexisting unions as part of the acquisition negotiations. This does not mean that Walmart does not engage in antiunionism across the globe—there is clear evidence that it does. But this antiunionism is confined to the limits set by each country's labor laws and regulatory frameworks (Bank Muñoz et al. forthcoming).

Finally, the United States is a large, politically varied country. Walmart grew in Southern states known for right to work policies that limited the ability of workers to unionize (see chapter 1). Owing to the relative decentralization of the United States and strength of state rights, the political consciousness and mobilization of workers varies greatly across the country. For example, Walmart has not been able to penetrate New York City, which has 25 percent union density (Milkman and Luce 2016) compared with only 10.9 percent union density in the United States as a whole. In general Walmart has had a difficult time opening retail stores in the country's urban centers. Furthermore, the scope of organizing Walmart in the United States with its 1.5 million workers and over 4,500 distinct stores is very different from organizing in a small country such as Chile.

It is therefore impressive that despite the odds, Walmart workers in the United States have attempted both traditional unionization and other types of organizing outside that framework. In the United States organizations such as OUR Walmart, Warehouse Workers United, and Warehouse Workers for Justice have been fighting for justice in Walmart's retail and warehouse operations. Although they have met limited success, their ongoing campaigns are crucial to eventually being in a position to win against Walmart. So far in the 2010s, the U.S. campaign has had a number of legal victories. For example, in 2016 an NLRB judge ruled that Walmart must reinstate and pay back wages for sixteen workers it fired for participation in a 2013 strike (Lopez 2014). In 2014, Warehouse Workers United scored a huge two-part victory against Schneider Logistics, a transport firm hired by Walmart and Walmart. First, a judge determined that Walmart could also be named in the lawsuit against Schneider Logistics, because it could be considered a joint employer. Previously, Walmart had argued that Schneider was a contractor so Walmart was not responsible for its workers. The second victory involved a US$21 million settlement, which Schneider had to pay to over 1,800 employees who had worked at its facility between 2001 and 2013 (Lopez 2014).

These victories are significant, but there is much more organizing to do. Unfortunately, the United Food and Commercial Workers Union (UFCW) has reduced its overall budget for organizing Walmart, leading to the dismantling of Warehouse Workers United. Furthermore, OUR Walmart has been mired in conflicts and has split from the UFCW. Some scholars have critiqued the UFCW's approach as top down and bureaucratic, making it difficult for workers to own their campaigns. OUR Walmart by contrast has been much more committed to building worker power from below, but with limited access to funds, it is a slow, if steady endeavor. Furthermore the election of Donald Trump as president of the United States creates as challenging and uncertain future for labor for both traditional unions and alternative models.

Institutional Context Matters

Despite Walmart's many efforts to impose its doctrine wholesale in its global operations, it has not succeeded. Instead, Walmart has had to learn flexibility and adjust its approach in different countries. An early rigidity in part explains Walmart's failures in Germany and Japan. When Walmart entered Germany in the 1990s, its model was met with resistance from unions, employer associations, small manufacturers, and farmers (Christopherson 2006). German workers were particularly averse to Walmart's cultural practices, such as the Walmart cheer, and clapping. Eventually, after four years of taking significant losses Walmart closed in Germany. In Japan, Walmart faced other challenges. It entered a market where supermarkets that combine food and nonfood items were on the decline. Whereas in the United States the model of combining supermarket and retail store was somewhat innovative, it had been a traditional feature of supermarkets in Japan. Furthermore, Walmart ran into problems with Japan's regulatory policies (Aoyama and Schwarz 2006). In addition to Germany and Japan, Walmart also failed in South Korea and Indonesia.

Walmart has been somewhat chastened by these international ventures and has been more careful in Chile and South Africa. Nonetheless, Walmart's approach in Chile has been to push the regulatory framework as much as it can, often engaging in illegal practices. For example, Walmart has been on the government's list of companies charged with illegal antiunion practices for many years (chapter 5). Still, Walmart had not only to accept the existing unions in Chile upon its acquisition of D&S but also to reckon with organizing campaigns of the Ekono stores after the acquisition. The transnational had to accept unions because of Chilean labor law, which allows the organization of workers into unions. Chilean labor law is complex because it changed significantly with the dictatorship, and there has been no substantive change to labor law in the twenty plus years of power of the Concertación governments (chapter 2). Before the dictatorship unions were organized both as enterprise level unions, and in some cases by sector, providing more structural power to unions. Today, unions are organized exclusively at the enterprise level, with no possibility of unions across enterprises (individual stores or factories) as long as the employer opposes it. This model has generally served to weaken the labor movement in Chile.

Turning Problematic Labor Law on Its Head

Although unanticipated or unintended consequences of Chilean labor law exist, they do not outweigh the need for labor-law reform that allows unions to organize by sector and have closed shops (where employees must join a union as a condition of employment). As long as Chilean unions are forced into an enterprise-level system, they will not be able to build the broad power they need to create societal changes that fundamentally shift inequality. Nonetheless, the unions in this book have made the most they could out of the existing industrial relations system.

First, the enterprise unions in this study have established and advanced union democracy. In their classic piece, Offe and Wiesenthal (1980) argue that unlike employer associations, unions face a dilemma: Their members must be willing to pay (membership dues), and they must be willing to act (go on strike). As unions attempt to increase their power (willingness to act), they tend to become bureaucratic. As they become more bureaucratic, a distance grows between the rank and file and leadership, which begins to rely on external sources of legitimacy and power (state policies). The problem with relying on external sources of power is that state policies change according to different political climates. Therefore in the end unions that become too bureaucratized and rely on external sources of power may end up in a bind and have to go back to the membership and rebuild power from the base. In short, more bureaucratization means less internal democracy for unions. Smaller organizations have more opportunities to practice union democracy (Dimick 2010).The key to a successful union is not only formal democracy and contested elections but democracy rooted in widespread membership participation and decision making. There are of course examples of large democratic unions. In the United States a good example is the United Electrical Workers Union. However, most large unions tend to be hierarchical and more bureaucratic. The Chilean autonomous unions have made the best of weak labor law protections and have taken advantage of their smaller and less bureaucratic organizations to create truly democratic unions.

Second, Chilean labor law allows for multiple unions to have a presence in one single enterprise or workplace. This policy is not unprecedented; many countries in the European Union allow this practice. Furthermore, this practice is supported under the International Labor Organization convention 87 on freedom of association. In reality the U.S. case of exclusive representation[1] is more the exception than the rule in this respect.

---

1. Exclusive representation refers to the right of a union to represent all members in a particular workplace to represent all employees in that workplace whether or not they are members of the union.

Of course exclusive representation gives unions more power vis-à-vis employers, because there is less opportunity to divide and conquer different factions. However, a number of scholars—including Lipset et al. (1956), Cohen and Rogers (1992), Baccaro (2006), and Dimick (2010)—point to the importance of secondary associations and workplace associations in cultivating union democracy. Dimick (2010) argues that secondary associations have the potential to strengthen democracy by generating new ideas, creating alternative networks, training new leaders, encouraging participation, and serving as a basis of opposition to centralized authority. When discussing secondary associations most of these scholars are specifically pointing to workplace associations within already existing unions, rather than multiple unions inside a workplace, as is the case with Chile. Few would question the value of suborganizations within unions that challenge union bureaucracy. In the United States an important example of this kind of organization is Teamsters for a Democratic Union, within the Teamsters union. When these kinds of organizations are strong, they can do a lot to hold their union leadership accountable.

In Chile the dynamic is more complicated, because the labor movement is already deeply fragmented. The fact that there are eighty-six different Walmart unions is a case in point. Allowing multiple unions in one workplace means that a store with say 200 employees can have three or more different unions, with different collective bargaining agreements and cultures. On the one hand, this circumstance forces the smaller unions to constantly organize, even between collective bargaining periods, to improve their working conditions. One of the biggest successes of the Sindicato Matucana, part of the Federación Autónoma, has been to become so powerful and relevant that many members of the other two unions at the Líder Matucana have left their unions to join Sindicato Matucana. Since this union is in constant organizing mode it has been able to recruit new members by leading by example.

On the other hand, it is extremely resource intensive to constantly be fighting a war on two or three fronts, against the boss and the two or three other unions in your workplace. Not only does it deplete energy for other organizing, but the constant fighting takes a toll on membership activists and fatigue sets in. Furthermore, Walmart has been expert at keeping the different union federations divided by appealing to the different leaders' styles and offering each federation something different in contract negotiations. In short there are costs and benefits to having multiple unions in one particular workplace. It does tend to keep unions accountable to the needs of their members. Accountability helps unions avoid the complacency that is common in leaders who are secure in their positions. Having multiple unions in one particular workplace also offers these unions the opportunity to develop more democratic structures as a way to expand their membership base. At the same time, it is challenging to use valuable resources to be constantly fighting on multiple fronts, especially when these unions do not have the large infrastructure that U.S. unions have. They do not have staff organizers, research departments, extensive access to legal resources, or a significant dues base.

Building Power from Below

The two most prominent characteristics of Chile's independent Walmart unions, both in retail and logistics, is their autonomy from the mainstream labor movement and political parties and their commitment to building democratic organizations. For these unions, building a democratic organization largely underlies their ability to develop strategic capacity. Interestingly, Ganz (2000, 2010) says nothing about the role of democratic organization in creating strategic capacity. Yet in the two retail federations and the warehouse union it is clear that democracy is intricately connected to strategic capacity. Strategic capacity relies on leaders' ability to experiment, access salient information, and deep motivation. Ganz further argues that variation in strategic capacity is produced by differences in "leaders' life experiences, networks and repertoires, and organizations' deliberative processes, resource flows, and accountability structures" (2000, 1005). Deliberative processes and accountability structures are of course related to democracy, but Ganz (2000, 2010) simply does not engage with union democracy as a concept in his work on strategic capacity.

The democratic structures that Chilean warehouse workers have built into their union have deepened their capacity for developing effective strategy. Leaders' life experiences, including prior union experience, antidictatorship organizing, as well as negative experiences with unions, shaped their commitment to building a "real" union. Because some of the warehouse workers had prior experience with social movements, they had a clear understanding of what they did and did not want to replicate in the union. Leaders also had greater access to salient information because they built a democratic union that prioritized political education and leadership development. As a result workers have significant control over the productive process, which closes the feedback loop on information. Leaders were also deeply motivated because they came directly from the rank and file. Whereas the union president receives release time for union work, committee members, including those on the executive committee, work full time on the shopfloor. As a result there is no distance between workers and leaders, with the exception of the president, and he is kept accountable by the executive committee, bylaws of the union, and the membership as a whole.

Similarly, the retail worker unions and federations have leaders with a wide variety of experiences that have shaped their organizations. Although they generally have less political experience than warehouse union leaders, they do have members who have been involved in political organizing or were previously members of other unions. Furthermore, these workers, many of them women, have had other formative experiences such as discrimination, sexual harassment, and abuse. They also have a clear sense of what they want to replicate and not replicate in their unions. Retail workers generally have less control over the productive process, and therefore different kinds of leverage from the warehouse union; however, they created an effective steward structure that is tapped into what is happening on the ground. They have built a flexible, militant, and highly responsive shopfloor culture. Finally, like the warehouse workers, these unionists have a deep sense of motivation and commitment to improving conditions at work and building their organizations.

Going Global? The Trials and Tribulations of Transnational Solidarity

Given that most of Walmart's global operations are unionized and that in some cases workers are actually winning and building powerful grassroots organizations, some have called for a global strategy to organize Walmart. It has been en vogue for some time now to call for a global labor movement and transnational solidarity as a counter to hegemonic globalization

(Anner 2011l; Anner and Evans 2004; Armbruster Sandoval 2004; Bronfenbrenner 2007; Evans 2008, 2010; Lerner 2007; McCallum 2013; Seidman 2007; Silver 2003,). Scholars have astutely and correctly identified the opportunity for labor to globalize in the face of increasingly few transnational corporations that dominate the global scene. However, the practice of a transnational or global strategy for labor is far more complicated than the call. As McCallum (2013) points out, few studies have actually observed the process of labor transnationalism on the ground. And from-the-ground transnational campaigns often seem overwhelming and daunting. Furthermore, there are many questions that need to be asked. Who benefits from a global labor strategy? Who are the decision makers? Who are the participants? How are local needs and varying institutional contexts taken into account? How are power differentials between workers in different countries managed? The case study of Chile offers some important reflections on the challenges for global labor.

UNI Global, UFCW, and Change to Win Come to Chile

The UFCW is the largest union representing retail, supermarket, and meat processing workers in the United States. It has been trying to organize Walmart since the 1990s, having little success in formally unionizing the transnational corporation. In its epic battle against Walmart the UFCW realized that a global strategy was imperative—after all a global Walmart movement could exert significant pressure on Walmart and eventually force the behemoth to recognize the union rights of U.S. workers. The organization put significant financial resources into such a strategy and partnered with Union Network International (UNI) Global Union, one of the largest global labor federations to challenge Walmart on a transnational scale.[2] During the time of my fieldwork in 2011, the UFCW and UNI were primarily working on developing a Global Framework Agreement (GFA) that they wanted to pressure Walmart to accept. GFAs are "nonbinding contracts signed between Global Union Federations (GUFs) and transnational corporations that attempt to secure labor standards throughout a company's operations, and in some cases, its supply chain" (McCallum

---

2. The UFCW is one of the largest unions that is a member organization of UNI.

2013, 37). They represent the first collective bargaining negotiations between global employers and unions in the history of the labor movement (McCallum 2013) and have become an important strategy for unions attempting to organize globally. However, like their predecessors—codes of conduct—GFAs have been critiqued for not reaching workers on the ground and potentially weakening local labor movements (Seidman 2008). McCallum (2013) challenges this notion, in his study of one of the most important GFAs negotiated between the Service Employees International Union (SEIU) and UNI and G4S, a global security company employing three-quarters of a million people in 125 countries (McCallum 2013). After a five-year campaign, G4S workers won the ability to organize unions without the threat of management reprisals, significantly changing their working conditions (McCallum 2013). Having had success with G4S,[3] UNI and the UFCW were hopeful that the GFA strategy could force Walmart to recognize workers' fundamental labor rights across the globe, and especially in the United States.

In addition to developing a GFA, the UFCW and UNI in partnership with the South African labor movement tried to block Walmart's entry into South Africa. The goal was to put enough pressure on the South African government through the competition tribunal[4] hearings to either block Walmart from the country or push for heavy restrictions on entry (see below).

The U.S. labor federation Change to Win (CTW) of which the UFCW is a member was also heavily involved in the Walmart campaign. CTW is one of two national labor federations in the United States. The more well-known federation is the American Federation of Labor and Congress of Industrial Organizations (AFL-CIO). In 2005 a group of unions including SEIU and the UFCW split away from the AFL-CIO, creating a new federation, Change to Win. As a member of UNI Global, CTW worked on a different aspect of the global Walmart campaign. It focused on the logistics sector and building capacity and transnational relationships in

---

3. The G4S campaign improved wages and working conditions in many places, it was also criticized as a movement driven from the top by SEIU and UNI. Furthermore. However, it is unclear how much SEIU gained from this global strategy, since in the end SEIU was only able to organize about 1,000 G4S workers in the United States.

4. The South African Competition Tribunal adjudicates on mergers and acquisitions.

that realm. When I first learned about the exciting organizing work happening at Walmart in Chile, I was eager to broker a relationship between these unions and the U.S. unions working on a global campaign against Walmart. Unfortunately, all too soon it became painfully clear how difficult these relationships would be.

To start, both the retail federations and the warehouse union were skeptical of U.S. unions, owing to the direct and indirect roles that U.S. unions had played in military coups across Latin America (Harding and Spalding 1976; Herod 1997; Shorrock 2003). In 1962, George Meany, then president of the AFL-CIO, created an international labor organization called the American Institute for Free Labor Development (AIFLD) (Anner 2011). The AIFLD board included heads of powerful corporations, as well as unions. The goal was to create a favorable business climate across the globe. The AIFLD, in part funded by and working with the CIA, helped overthrow democratically elected leaders in Brazil, Chile, and the Dominican Republic. In Chile, the AIFLD worked with the CIA to pour millions of dollars into right-wing parties opposing Salvador Allende's candidacy. Then the organization worked with transportation and communications unions in Chile to clear the path for the military coup (Shorrock 2003).

Needless to say, the autonomous unions I was working with had significant distrust of U.S. unions in general. By contrast, the U.S. unions, particularly the UFCW, were skeptical about the strategic capacity of these independent unions, basing their ideas on information gathered in meetings of the mainstream Chilean labor movement. Nonetheless, both the Chilean and U.S. unions were curious about each other and were interested in understanding the work that each was doing to challenge Walmart. The first step was to establish a trusting relationship. The first few months of the emergent relationship between the U.S. and Chilean unions was better than expected. Chilean workers expressed enthusiasm at the global campaign against Walmart. Both warehouse and retail unions were firm believers in labor internationalism, linking it to Marx's famous instruction "Workers of the World, Unite!"

South African Tribunal Process   The first opportunity for solidarity between the Chilean and U.S. unions came through the South African Tribunal process. In September 2010, a short year and a half after the purchase of D&S in Chile by Walmart, Walmart offered to purchase Massmart, South Africa's second leading retailer (Clifford 2010). In February 2011, South Africa held competition hearings to ensure that the purchase of Massmart by Walmart was in the public interest (Kenny 2014). During the course of the competition hearings, South African unions and the state voiced their concerns over the entry of Walmart into South Africa. Chief among those complaints was Walmart's history of antiunionism and creation of low-wage jobs. The UFCW and UNI were instrumental in helping the South African unions with legal resources (Kenny 2014). Furthermore, the UFCW was critical in getting unions from different countries to submit affidavits and provide testimony in the hearings documenting the abuses and antiunion behavior of Walmart in its global operations. Walmart for its part also brought in the global corporate heads of its operations to testify on its partnerships with unions in the Global South. Walmart Chile was put forth as the shining star in Walmart's global labor relations. Then CEO of Walmart Chile, Enrique Ostalé, testified. He argued that Walmart Chile employees were mostly happy with their jobs (based on an opinion poll paid for by the company), that Walmart had eliminated compulsory pregnancy testing, and that it had increased the overall number of jobs by eight percent in only three years (Ostalé 2011).

The independent Chilean Walmart labor unions responded both verbally and in an affidavit from their umbrella organization, the Consejo de Trabajadores Walmart Chile (Council of Chilean Walmart Workers). Some members of the Consejo flew to South Africa and testified on behalf of Walmart workers. The Consejo also drafted a written testimony responding to management's arguments that working at Walmart was a fantastic opportunity. The document presented countless examples of workplace abuses and antiunion tactics. The Consejo criticized the Walmart opinion survey, arguing that it was invalid because workers were intimidated and harassed until they filled it out. Furthermore, the Consejo unions forcefully stated that while compulsory pregnancy tests were eliminated, compulsory drug tests were newly mandated for Ekono workers, who had recently gone on strike. They also challenged the idea that the total number of employees had increased, since there was a shift from full-time work under D&S to increased precarious part-time employment under

Walmart (González Santibáñez and Consejo de Trabajadores Walmart Chile 2011).

Ultimately, the tribunal allowed Walmart to purchase Massmart with conditions. This decision was a victory for the UFCW, UNI, and the South African unions, because initially Walmart had been granted access to South Africa without any conditions. In order to purchase Massmart, Walmart had to rehire 500 workers that Massmart had fired, respect the labor contract with South African unions for three years, and contribute funds to a supplier program that would aid Black farmers. The program was to be controlled by a committee representing the South African government, South African unions, and Walmart.

The tribunal process was a great opportunity for the independent Chilean unions to get to know the UFCW and vice versa. Though it was a short-term collaboration, it was one that helped build some level of trust between the UFCW and the autonomous unions who were members of the Consejo. Furthermore, the Chilean unions were happy to work with the legendary unions in South Africa in their fight to stop Walmart from entering South Africa. They saw this as an opportunity to build transnational solidarity against a common global employer.

UNI, the UFCW, and the Chilean Retail Federations

As months passed, the relationship between the U.S. and Chilean unions became more complicated, in large part because their goals were different. Between 2011 and 2013 the relationship between the UFCW and the retail unions fractured and all but disappeared, but the relationship between CTW and the LTS had more lasting power.

The period after the South African competition hearings was challenging for the relationship between UNI, the UFCW, and the two autonomous retail federations for a number of reasons. There was significant pressure on behalf of the UFCW to get the FENATRALID to join UNI Global. For a long time the president of FENATRALID resisted the pressure to join UNI. Natalia Duque had many concerns about how an affiliation with UNI would help her organization and organizing Walmart workers in Chile generally (Natalia Duque 2011). She was particularly concerned that the president of the corrupt Sindicato Interempresa Lider (SIL) was also a member of UNI. She felt skeptical of any organization, especially a large international organization, that invited a fraudulent union leader to the table. UNI explained that this other trade union leader had become a member through official channels because he was a member of the CUT, Chile's equivalent to the AFL-CIO. Members of the UFCW argued that this was her opportunity to play an important role in showing UNI that her organization better represented the interests of workers. Eventually she joined UNI, with the hopes that she could be involved in building ties between Chilean workers and workers across the globe in their common interest of fighting Walmart. As a result of her membership she was flown to various places in Latin America and the United States to meet with other Walmart unions and attend UNI meetings. Within two years of her participation in UNI, she became disheartened and disillusioned with the organization, as it became clear that UNI wanted all the Chilean unions to work together and support the GFA. To the UFCW and UNI, the major political differences and forms of trade union organization between her federation and the corrupt SIL were chalked to petty internal strife that was undermining the Chilean labor movement (Natalia, interview 2011, 2013; Sandra, interview 2013). UNI pushed hard to pursue a strategy of union cooperation. Seeing that Natalia could not convince UNI to support the autonomous unions, the FENATRALID eventually pulled out of the international organization.

Furthermore, Natalia had many concerns about the strategy for a GFA and the role that UNI was playing in trying to find common ground between two dramatically different types of trade union organizations (Natalia, interview 2012). Since Chilean workers were actually making progress vis-à-vis Walmart, she felt that the GFA could potentially hurt the organizing efforts in Chile. For example, would the GFA offer a lower standard than workers had fought to establish in Chile? Would the GFA mimic the *acuerdo marco* (pattern agreement) that had been negotiated between Walmart and the SIL union? If so, this would undermine the years of work it took for the autonomous unions to break the pattern. She was also concerned that this movement for a GFA was driven by a large international organization and U.S. unions and not by Walmart unions themselves.

At the same time that the UFCW was pushing the FENATRALID to join UNI, it was also establishing its own independent relationship with the FENATRALID and the Federación Autónoma. In an attempt to generate goodwill the UFCW offered the Chilean organizations resources, but these were only for very specific things that interested the UFCW. For example, the UFCW wanted to fund a Chilean version of Walmart Watch, a website that existed in the United States as a watchdog organization for Walmart's bad labor practices. The hope was that Chilean workers could use the platform to report workplace abuses and antiunion actions. Such reports would help promote both worker and consumer education about Walmart's practices in Chile, and would also serve the global campaign. Chilean workers were not interested in the website idea. For starters, they pointed out that many workers did not have access to computers and did not consistently rely on the Internet for their source of information. The retail federations didn't see how this website would help them build power on the ground in Chile or anywhere else.

Instead the Chilean retail unionists proposed establishing direct relationships with retail workers in the United States and creating an exchange where U.S. workers would visit to learn how Chilean workers were fighting Walmart and Chilean workers would travel to the United States to see how U.S. workers were organizing. However, the UFCW saw this exchange as being resource intensive with little payback. The autonomous federations also sought funding for organizing activity to force the SIL union out of their stores and recruit SIL members into their unions. In the United States such activity would be akin to raiding a union for its membership, but in Chile it is not exactly raiding since multiple unions are allowed in one workplace. Nonetheless direct resources for organizing would put the UFCW in a politically uncomfortable situation, since it did not want to interfere in factional fights and particularly because the president of the SIL was a member of UNI. Eventually, the organizations went their separate ways, and no resources were contributed to the retail organizations. Over the course of the next few years, the UFCW occasionally reached out to the autonomous retail federations and asked for letters of solidarity from the Chilean unions, when for example, workers at U.S. Walmart stores were fired or engaged in actions such as the Black Friday strikes that started in 2012. Chilean unions always agreed to participate in these solidarity efforts. However, the relationship between the unions and the UFCW has largely fizzled. In 2016 UNI tried again to bring different federations together to work on concrete issues in Chile and provided a stipend for participating federations (Sandra, interview, 2016), but it is too soon to tell if anything will come of this new attempt at relationship building.

Change to Win and the Warehouse Union

The relationship between the CTW and the LTS was a slightly more optimistic story. While the UFCW was establishing its relationship with the retail unions, CTW, through its warehouse workers division was establishing a relationship with LTS. Over the course of several years these two organizations developed a more flexible and productive relationship than the retail unions and UFCW. Whereas the UFCW went into its relationship with the retail unions with clear goals, mostly uninterested in the unions' strategies, and with a prejudice that its global strategy was most effective, the CTW took a different approach. The representative from the CTW expressed enthusiasm and genuine interest in learning about how the warehouse workers had achieved their gains. He was interested in LTS's approach, history, and movement-building strategy. In meetings between LTS and CTW, the CTW representative asked thoughtful questions and took a measured and slow approach to building trust. Over the course of several visits to Chile and meetings with LTS, the CTW representative presented relevant information about the global logistics industry and asked LTS how CTW could support LTS's efforts. CTW was particularly interested in helping LTS organize the nonunion warehouse that Walmart had opened in 2012.

As a result of building this relationship, CTW provided LTS with financial resources and gave LTS the flexibility to use those resources however it saw fit. CTW believed that providing some financial resources would generate goodwill such that it could call on LTS for solidarity in the future. Furthermore, CTW trusted that LTS would use the resources wisely and productively. LTS was initially skeptical of receiving resources (Rodrigo, interview 2012), because it feared that the U.S. union would use the gift to interfere in LTS operations. Leaders also hesitated to accept the funds because they were unclear how the membership and union activists would react to financial resources coming from a U.S. union. In particular, the executive committee was afraid that members would become complacent and possibly less involved if they knew that the union was well financed from the outside (González Santibáñez 2012). LTS ultimately did accept CTW's offer. LTS drafted a proposal for organizing the nonunion warehouse, and CTW wired the funds in several installments. Over the course of a year and a half, LTS developed a relationship with workers in the nonunion warehouse and those workers eventually organized their own union, and negotiated their first contract in 2016.

What did the CTW get out of its relationship with LTS? Part of the reason that LTS grew to trust CTW was that CTW expected little from it, except an ongoing commitment to doing good work. The representative from CTW had a long view of the campaign and felt that helping build strong Chilean unions would benefit warehouse workers around the world. Nonetheless, CTW did call on LTS for help and solidarity. For example, in 2013 when Walmart fired California logistics workers involved in a worker center east of Los Angeles, the LTS union sent a video of solidarity and support. Over the course of several months it also sent other statements and messages of support. Furthermore, the CTW representative brought back information to the United States about how LTS controlled production and organized its union. The representative shared the strategy of mapping production. In short, the humility, resources, and flexibility with which the CTW approached its relationship with LTS led to more trust, longer engagement, and a project that was seen to benefit both the Chilean unions and CTW.

There were of course some sticking points in the relationship. Like the two retail federations, LTS was interested in some kind of worker-to-worker exchange, where they could meet and discuss common goals and learn from each other. However, CTW was not interested in funding this kind of exchange, for similar reasons as the UFCW. It felt the initiative would be resource intensive without any clear take away. CTW was also interested in having LTS join the International Transport Workers' Federation (ITF). However, LTS was skeptical about the role of international labor federations in its union. In addition, LTS had periods of non-responsiveness where it was difficult to facilitate communication between the organizations. Nonetheless, because they had already established a trusting relationship, CTW and LTS were able to weather these tensions and differences.

In 2014, Joseph Hansen, the president of the UFCW responsible for directing union resources to the Walmart campaign, retired. The executive board of the union voted to replace him with Anthony Perrone, then secretary treasurer of the union. Four months into Perrone's term the UFCW dramatically reduced funding to the Walmart campaign. The shake-up in the union had led to changes in its structure and priorities. In particular, the reduction in funds for the campaign eliminated CTW's warehouse division and created tensions that divided the UFCW and one part of the OUR Walmart organization (Moberg 2015; Olney 2015). As a result of these changes in the UFCW and CTW, by 2014 there was no longer a relationship between Chilean logistics workers and U.S. logistics workers.

Lessons Learned

In the example of Chile we have a set of complicated relationships. The UFCW came to Chile with a specific set of hopes and expectations. It was somewhat rigid about the kind of relationship it wanted to build with the independent Chilean retail unions, and it was also constrained by its ties to UNI. As a result, not much came out of the relationship between the UFCW and retail unions. At best the retail unions viewed the UFCW as a traditional union that was not committed to base building or creating serious transnational relationships. These unions continue to distrust UNI's efforts, especially since the leader of the SIL has become more influential in that organization. Perhaps that will change with the recent UNI initiative to build collective work projects between UNI and Chile's various union federations.

By contrast, CTW came into Chile with no expectations, some resources, flexibility, and a genuine interest in learning from Chilean workers. It generated goodwill and established a relationship that was challenging but functional. As a result of this relationship LTS was able to organize Walmart's nonunion warehouse and show solidarity with U.S. warehouse workers. Most importantly it was a relationship that would have likely continued had the UFCW not cut funding from the Walmart campaign.

The experiences of Chilean workers with UNI, UFCW, and CTW illustrate the many challenges of creating a global labor movement, and I have focused on the complications in only one country. There is no question that we must find ways to overcome the challenges faced by a global unions; yet we simultaneously must be cautious about how we establish relationships and partnerships. Unions need to be humble in their approach to global work, especially when it is initiated by unions in the Global North. The painful history of the role of U.S. unions in the Global South cannot simply be wished away. We must be attuned to the needs and histories of workers across the globe. In some countries it might make sense to push for Global Framework Agreements, in other countries it might not—in fact, it might be damaging. There are no one size fits all solutions in our increasingly complex world. What makes these dynamics even more complicated is that the individuals in these institutions all have good intentions. The representatives that I met and worked with in the UFCW, UNI, and CTW were all hard working people committed to improving the lives of workers. Nonetheless, it is not always enough to have good intentions. Sometimes organizational histories and institutional bureaucracies get in the way of these good intentions despite our best efforts. This is why a critical analysis of the labor movement both from within and outside of it is imperative to move forward in understanding and overcoming the challenges of global labor solidarity.

In this book I have argued for the centrality of union democracy, militancy, and strategic capacity in building strong associational power and thereby augmenting unions' capacity for disruption. In order for global unions to effectively disrupt business as usual for transnational corporations, they must be comprised of organizations that are connected with their membership bases and engaged in democratic decision making. If U.S. unions and international organizations are initiating global solidarity for their purposes alone and setting the agenda only on their terms, then the movement is doomed to failure. If on the other hand, the different actors each benefit from the relationship, learn from each other, successfully negotiate the challenges posed by different cultures, interests, and institutional contexts, work humbly and slowly, then we might have an opportunity to create a global labor movement with the capacity to disrupt transnational capital.

REFERENCES

Adkins, Lisa. 1995. *Gendered Work: Sexuality, Family, and the Labour Market.* London: Open University Press.

Anner, Mark. 2011. *Solidarity Transformed: Labor Responses to Globalization and Crisis in Latin America.* Ithaca: Cornell University Press.

Anner, Mark, and Peter Evans. 2004. "Building Bridges across a Double Divide: Alliances between U.S. and Latin American Labour and NGOs." *Development in Practice* 14(1–2): 34–47.

Angell, Alan. 1972. *Politics and the Labour Movement in Chile.* London: Oxford University Press.

Aoyama, Yuko, and Guido Schwarz. 2006. "The Myth of Walmartization: Retail Globalization and Local Competition in Japan and Germany." In *Wal-Mart World: The World's Biggest Corporation,* edited by Stanley D. Brunn, 275–93. New York: Routledge.

Álvarez Vallejos, Rolando. 2009. "Desde Fuera o Dentro de la Institucionalidad? La 'Huelga Larga del Salmón' y Las Nuevas Estrategias Sindicales en Chile (2006–2008)." In *El Renacer de la Huelga Obrera en Chile: El Movimiento Sindical en la Primera Década del Siglo XXI,* edited by Antonio Aravena and Daniel Núñez, 75–116. Santiago: Instituto de Ciencias Alejandro Lipschultz.

Araujo, Kathya, and Danilo Martuccelli. 2012. *Desafíos Comunes: Retrato de la Sociedad Chilena y sus Individuales.* Vol. 1. Santiago: LOM Editoriales.

Aravena, Antonio, and Daniel Núñez, eds. 2009. *El Renacer de la Huelga Obrera en Chile: El Movimiento Sindical en la Primera Década del Siglo XXI.* Santiago: Instituto de Ciencias Alejandro Lipschultz.

Armbruster Sandoval, Ralph. 2004. *Globalization and Cross-Border Labor Solidarity in the Americas: The Anti-Sweatshop Movement and the Struggle for Social Justice.* New York: Routledge.

Armstrong, Alberto J., and Rafael A. Águila. 2006. *Evolución del Conflicto Laboral en Chile 1961–2002.* Santiago: Pontificia Universidad Católica de Chile.

Armstrong, Alberto J., and Rafael A. Águila. 2011. "Evolución de Huelgas Laborales en Chile, 1979–2009." *Administración y Economía.* 69: 13–17. Santiago: Ediciones Universidad Católica de Chile.

Artaza Barrios, Pablo. 1998. *A 90 Años de los Sucesos de la Escuela Santa María de Iquique.* Santiago: LOM Ediciones.

Baccaro, Lucio. 2006. "Union Democracy and the Italian Labor Movement." Paper presented at the Conference on Union Democracy Re-Examined, University of Washington.

Bank Muñoz, Carolina. 2008. *Transnational Tortillas: Race, Gender, and Shop-Floor Politics in Mexico and the United States.* Ithaca: Cornell University Press.

Bank Muñoz, Carolina, Bridget Kenny, and Antonio Stetcher, eds. Forthcoming. *Walmart in the Global South: State Regulation, Labor Politics, and Local Cultures.* Austin: University of Texas Press.

Barrera, Mario, and Julio Valenzuela. 1987. "The Development of Labor Movement Opposition to the Military Regime." In *Military Rule in Chile: Dictatorship and Oppositions*, edited by Julio Valezuela and Arturo Valenzuela, pp. 170–230. Baltimore: Johns Hopkins University Press.

Barrionuevo, Alexei. 2011. "Rise of Consumer Credit in Chile and Brazil Leads to Big Debts and Lender Abuse." *New York Times,* July 23. Accessed November 19, 2013. http://www.nytimes.com/2011/07/24/business/global/abuses-by-credit-issuers-in-chile-and-brazil-snare-consumers.html?_r=0.

Best, Dean. 2011. "CHILE: Wal-Mart Eyes Expansion." *Just Food,* April 21. Accessed March 30, 2014. http://www.just-food.com/news/wal-mart-eyes-expansion_id115036.aspx.

Boorstein, Edward. 1977. *Allende's Chile: An Inside View.* New York: International Publishers.

Bronfenbrenner, Kate, ed. 2007. *Global Unions: Challenging Transnational Capital through Cross-Border Campaigns.* Ithaca: Cornell University Press.

Bronfenbrenner, Kate, and Sheldon Friedman, eds. 1998. *Organizing to Win: New Research on Union Strategies.* Ithaca: Cornell University Press.

Berfield, Susan. 2015. "How Walmart Keeps an Eye on its Massive Workforce: The Retail Giant Is Always Watching." *Bloomberg Businessweek,* November 24.

Bonacich, Edna, and Jake Wilson. 2008. *Getting the Goods: Ports, Labor, and the Logistics Revolution.* Ithaca: Cornell University Press.

Brown, Jenny. 2011. "Store Workers Say: Whose Wal-Mart? OUR Wal-Mart." *Labor Notes,* August 28.

Burawoy, Michael. 1979. *Manufacturing Consent: Changes in the Labor Process under Monopoly Capitalism*. Chicago: University of Chicago Press.

Bureau of Labor Statistics. "Strike Report." Accessed December 21, 2016. https://www.bls.gov/ces/cesstrk.htm.

Calderon Hoffman, Alvaro. 2006. "The Expansion Model of the Major Chilean Retail Chains." *Cepal Review* 90: 149–68.

Campusano, Karim. 2015. *Desmistificando la Huelga Legal. Reflexiones sobre la Conflictividad Sindical en el Sector Servicios, Financiero y Comerico*. Santiago: Centro de Investigación Político Social del Trabajo.

Casanova, Erynn. 2011. *Making up the Difference: Women, Beauty, and Direct Selling in Ecuador*. Austin: University of Texas Press.

——. 2013. "Embodied Inequality: The Experience of Domestic Work in Urban Ecuador." *Gender and Society* 27(4): 561–85.

Chan, Anita, ed. 2011. *Walmart in China*. Ithaca: ILR Press.

Chile. 2012. "Annual Report." Accessed June 12, 2013. http://memoria.walmartchile.cl/2012/Memoria-WalmartChile-2012.pdfmemorial.

Chun, Jennifer. 2009. *Organizing at the Margins: The Symbolic Politics of Labor in South Korea and the United States*. Ithaca: Cornell University Press.

Christopherson, Susan. 2006. "Challenges Facing Wal-Mart in the German Market." In *Wal-Mart World: The World's Biggest Corporation in the Global Economy*, edited by Stanley D. Brunn, 261–75. New York: Routledge.

Clifford, Stephanie. 2010. "Walmart Bids for Massmart to Expand into Africa. *New York Times*, September 27. Accessed February 12, 2014. http://www.nytimes.com/2010/09/28/business/global/28walmart.html.

Cohen, Joshua, and Joel Rogers. 1992. "Secondary Associations and Democratic Governance." *Politics and Society* 20(4): 393–472.

Cohn, Samuel. 1993. *When Strikes Make Sense—And Why: Lessons from Third Republic French Coals Miners*. Berlin: Springer Science & Business Media.

Collins, Joseph, and John Lear. 1995. *Chile's Free-Market Miracle: A Second Look*. Oakland: Institute for Food Development and Policy.

Constable, Pamela, and Arturo Valenzuela. 1991. *A Nation of Enemies: Chile Under Pinochet*. New York: W.W. Norton.

Cook, Alice. 1963. *Union Democracy: Practice and Ideal: An Analysis of Four Large Local Unions*. Ithaca: Cornell University Press.

Court of Appeals San Miguel. 2011. "Ruling against Wal-Mart for Monopoly Violations." Rol No. 130-2011.

Court of Appeals. 2009. Rol N° 159-2011.

Dimick, Matthew. 2010. "Revitalizing Union Democracy: Labor Law, Bureaucracy, and Workplace Association." *Denver Law Review* 88(1): 1–56.

Dirección del Trabajo, Gobierno de Chile. 2009. *Empresas Condenadas Por Prácticas Antisindicales*. Accessed July 14, 2011. www.dt.gob.cl/1601/articles-94445_recurso_22_pdf.

——. 2011. *Empresas Condenadas Por Prácticas Antisindicales*. Accessed December 16, 2011. www.dt.gob.cl/1601/articles-94445_recurso_22_pdf.

——. 2012a. *Código del Trabajo.* Accessed July 14, 2014. http://www.dt.gob.cl/legislacion/1611/articles-95516_recurso_1.pdf

——. 2012b. *Empresas Condenadas Por Prácticas Antisindicales.* Accessed June 13, 2013. www.dt.gob.cl/1601/articles-94445_recurso_22_pdf.

——. 2014. "Capítulo 1: Organizaciones Sindicales." In *Compendio Estadístico 2014.* Accessed September 15, 2016. http://www.dt.gob.cl/documentacion/1612/articles-62614_recurso_1.pdf.

——. 2015. *Empresas Condenadas Por Prácticas Antisindicales.* Accessed July 14, 2016. www.dt.gob.cl/1601/articles-94445_recurso_22_pdf.

——. 2016. *Empresas Condenadas Por Prácticas Antisindicales.* Accessed September 16, 2016. www.dt.gob.cl/1601/articles-94445_recurso_22_pdf.

Distribución y Servicios (D&S). *Historia de DyS.* Accessed May 21, 2014. http://www.dys.cl.

Dornbusch, Rudiger, and Sebastian Edwards. 1992. "The Macroeconomics of Populism." In *The Macroeconomics of Populism in Latin America,* edited by Sebastian Edwards and Rudiger Dornbusch, pp. 7–13. Chicago: University of Chicago Press.

Drake, Paul, W. 1996. *Labor Movements and Dictatorships.* Baltimore: John Hopkins University Press.

Dube, Arindrajit, and Ken Jacobs. 2004. *Hidden Cost of Wal-Mart Jobs: Use of Safety Net programs by Wal-Mart Workers in California.* Berkeley: Center for Labor Research and Education, Institute of Industrial Relations, University of California.

Dubofsky, Melvyn. 1995. "Labor Unrest in the United States, 1906–90." *Review* 18: 125–35.

Durán, Gonzalo. 2011. "Instalacíon de Wal-Mart en Chile: Interrogando la Modernizacion de Retail Desde la Perspectiva de los Trabajadores." Paper presented at the Walmart Conference at the Universidad Diego Portales.

Durán, Gonzalo, and Marco Kremerman. 2008. *Caracterización del Sector Retail: Una Mirada General.* Santiago: Fundacion Sol.

——. 2015a. *Sindicatos y Negociación Collectiva: Panorama Estadístico Nacional y Evidencia Comparada.* Santiago: Fundacion Sol.

——. 2015b. *Los Verdaderos Sueldos en Chile: Panorama Actual del Valor del Trabajo Usando la Encuesta NESI.* Santiago: Fundacion Sol.

Echeverría, Magdalena. 2010. *La Historía Inconclusa de la Subcontratación y el Relato de los Trabajadores.* Santiago: Dirección de Trabajo.

Edelstein, David, and Malcolm Warner. 1976. *Comparative Union Democracy: Organisation and Opposition in British and American Unions.* New Brunswick, NJ: Transaction Publishers.

Eidelson, Josh. 2012. "With Biggest Strike, Against Biggest Employer, Wal-Mart Workers Make History Again." *The Nation,* November 24.

"El 'Sucio de DyS.' " 2007. *La Nación,* October 28. Accessed April 12, 2011. http://www.lanacion.cl/noticias/vida-y-estilo/el-sucio-de-d-s/2007-10-28/003600.html.

Evans, Peter. 2008. "Is an Alternative Globalization Possible?" *Politics & Society* 36(2): 271–305.

——. 2010. "Is It Labor's Turn to Globalize? Twenty-First Century Opportunities and Strategic Responses." *Global Labour Journal* 1(3). https://escarpmentpress.org/globallabour/article/view/1082.

Frank, Volker. 2004. "Politics without Policy: The Failure of Social Concertation in Democratic Chile, 1990–2000." In *Victims of the Chilean Miracle: Workers and Neoliberalism in the Pinochet Era, 1973–2002*, edited by Peter Winn, pp. 71–124. Durham: Duke University Press.

——. 2015. "Living in the Past or Living with the Past? Reflections on Chilean Labor Unions Twenty Years into Democracy." In *Working through the Past: Labor and Authoritarian Legacies in Comparative Perspective*, edited by Teri L. Caraway, Maria Lorena Cook, and Stephen Crowley, pp. 179–96. Ithaca: Cornell University Press.

Ganz, Marshall. 2000. "Resources and Resourcefulness: Strategic Capacity in the Unionization of California Agriculture, 1959–1966." *American Journal of Sociology* 105(4):1003–62.

——. 2010. *Why David Sometimes Wins: Leadership, Organization, and Strategy in the California Farm Worker Movement*. London: Oxford University Press.

Gariazzo, Alicia. 2007. "La Industria del Retail en Chile y el Modelo Wal-Mart." Sección de Economía, Camara de Diputados Working Paper. Accessed August 11, 2011. http://www.carlosmontes.cl/senador/wp-content/uploads/documentos/privatizaciones/la-industria-del-retail-en-chile.pdf.

Gaudichaud, Franck. 2015. *Las Fisuras del Neoliberalismo Chileno: Trabajo, Crisis de la "Democracia Tutelada" y Conflictos de Clases*. Santiago: Quimantú y Tiempo Robado Editoras.

González Santibáñez, Cristián. 2012. "A Propósito Dos Fallos por Conductas Antisindicales de Walmart—Chile." Unpublished Report.

González Santibáñez, Cristián, and Consejo de Trabajadores Walmart Chile. 2011. "El (Mal) Trato Laboral de Walmart en Chile." Unpublished Report.

Gramsci, Antonio. 1919. "Unions and Councils." Trans. Michael Carley. *L'Ordine Nuovo*, October 11. Accessed December 29, 2016. https://www.marxists.org/archive/gramsci/1919/10/unions-councils.htm.

Greenwald, Richard. 2005. *The Triangle Fire, Protocols of Peace and Industrial Democracy in Progressive Era New York*. Philadelphia: Temple University Press.

Gutiérrez Crocco, Francisca, and Ignacio Gutiérrez Crocco. 2015. "Judicializar para generar cambios sociales? La discreta acción de la Dirección de Trabajo y el Poder Judicial en la erosion de la institucionalidad laboral de la dictadura en Chile." Working Paper, Universidad Alberto Hurtado.

Harding, Timothy F., and Hobart A. Spalding. 1976. "The Struggle Sharpens: Workers, Imperialism and the State in Latin America: Common Themes and New Directions." *Latin American Perspectives* 3(1): 3–14.

Harmer, Tanya. 2014. *Allende's Chile and the Inter-American Cold War*. Chapel Hill: University of North Carolina Press.

Harvey, David. 2005. *A Brief History of Neoliberalism*. London: Oxford University Press.

Herod, Andrew. 1997. "Labor as an Agent of Globalization and as a Global Agent." In *Spaces of Globalization: Reasserting the Power of the Local*, edited by Kevin R. Cox, pp. 167–200. New York: Guilford Press.

Hickey, Robert, Sarosh Kuruvilla, and Tashlin Lakhani. 2010. "No Panacea for Success: Member Activism, Organizing and Union Renewal." *British Journal of Industrial Relations* 48(1): 53–83.

Hípermercado Líder Matucana. 2011. "Disculpas Pblicas." Apology letter issued by Walmart Management.

Human Rights Watch. 2007. *U.S. Wal-Mart Denies Workers Basic Rights: Weak Labor Laws Perpetuate Abuses*. Report, April 30. Accessed July 14, 2013. https://www.hrw.org/news/2007/04/30/us-wal-mart-denies-workers-basic-rights.

Instituto Nacional de Estadísticas. "Estadísticas Electorales." 2011. Accessed July 16, 2015. http://www.ine.cl/canales/menu/publicaciones/compendio_estadistico/pdf/2011/1.9 estadisticas_electorales.pdf.

Isaac, Larry, and Lars Christiansen. 2002. "How the Civil Rights Movement Revitalized Labor Militancy." *American Sociological Review* 67(5): 722–46.

Jenkins, Steve. 2002. "Organizing, Advocacy, and Member Power." *Working USA* 6(2): 56–89.

Kenny, Bridget. 2014. "How Global? Wal-Mart and Labour Conditions in South Africa." Paper presented at the International Sociological Association, Yokohama, Japan, July 13–19.

Klein, Naomi. 2008. *The Shock Doctrine: The Rise of Disaster Capitalism*. New York: Picador.

Klubock, Thomas Miller. 2004. "Class, Community, and Neoliberalism in Chile: Copper Workers and the Labor Movement during the Military Dictatorship and the Restoration of Democracy." In *Victims of the Chilean Miracle: Workers and Neoliberalism in the Pinochet Era, 1973–2002*, pp. 209–60. Durham: Duke University Press.

Kornbluh, Peter. 2003. *The Pinochet File: A Declassified Dossier on Atrocity and Accountability*. New York: New Press.

Kroll, Andy. 2013. "Wal-Mart Workers Get Organized, Just Don't Say the U-word." *Mother Jones* March/April. http://www.motherjones.com/politics/2013/02/our-walmart-black-friday-union

Leiva, Fernando. 2012. "Flexible Workers, Gender, and Contending Strategies for Confronting the Crisis of Labor in Chile." *Latin American Perspectives* 39(4): 102–28.

——. 2013. "Chile's Labor Movement, 1990–2012: Ensnared in the Past and Absent from the Struggles to Democratize Society?" Paper presented at the Latin American Studies Congress, Washington DC.

Lerner, Stephen. 2007. "Global Unions: A Solution to Labor's Worldwide Decline." *New Labor Forum* 16(1): 23–37.

Lévesque, Christian, Gregor Murray, and Stephane Le Queux. 2005. "Union Disaffection and Social Identity Democracy as a Source of Union Revitalization." *Work and Occupations* 32(4): 400–422.

Levi, Margaret, David Olson, Jon Agnone, and Devin Kelly. 2009. "Union Democracy Reexamined." *Politics & Society* 37(2): 203–28.

Lichtenstein, Nelson. 1995. *Walter Reuther: The Most Dangerous Man in Detroit*. Chicago: University of Illinois Press.

——, ed. 2006. *Wal-Mart: The Face of Twenty-First Century Capitalism*. New York: New Press.

——. 2007. "How Wal-Mart Fights Unions." *Minnesota Law Review* 92:1462–1501.

——. 2010. *The Retail Revolution: How Wal-Mart Created a Brave New World of Business*. New York: Picador.

Lipset, Seymour Martin, Martin A. Trow, and James Samuel Coleman. 1956. *Union Democracy: The Internal Politics of the International Typographical Union.* Glencoe: Free Press.

López, Diego. 2007. *Labour Relations in Chile.* Amsterdam: Labor Again Publications.

Lopez, Ricardo. 2014. "Worker Win $21-Million Settlement Against Wal-Mart, Warehouses." *Los Angeles Times.* May 14.

Negociación Colectiva Ekono [Ekono Collective Bargaining Agreement]. 2012.

Negociación Colectiva Federación Autónoma [Autonomous Federation Collective Bargaining Agreement]. 2012.

———. 2015.

Negociación Colectiva FENATRALID [FENATRALID Federation Collective Bargaining Agreement]. 2014.

Negociación Colectiva LTS [LTS Collective Bargaining Agreement]. 2006.

———. 2008.

———. 2011.

Lynn, Barry C. 2006. "Breaking the Chain." *Harper's Magazine* 33: 29–36.

Markowitz, Linda. 1998. "After the Organizing Ends: Workers, Self-Efficacy, Activism, and Union Frameworks." *Social Problems* 45(3): 356–82.

———. 1999. *Worker Activism after Successful Union Organizing.* New York: Routledge.

Martínez, Javier, and Alvaro Díaz. 1996. *Chile: The Great Transformation.* Washington, DC: Brookings Institution Press.

Mattera, Philip, and Anna Purinton. 2004. *Shopping for Subsidies: How Wal-Mart Uses Taxpayer Money to Finance Its Never Ending Growth.* Washington, DC: Good Jobs First Institute.

McCallum, Jamie K. 2013. *Global Unions, Local Power: The New Spirit of Transnational Labor Organizing.* Ithaca: Cornell University Press.

McDowell, Linda. 1995. "Body Work: Heterosexual Gender Performances in City Workplaces." In *Mapping Desire: Geographies of Sexualities,* edited by David Bell and Gill Valentine, 75–95. London: Routledge.

———. 2009. *Working Bodies: Interactive Service Employment and Workplace Identities.* London: John Wiley & Sons.

Milkman, Ruth, ed. 2000. *Organizing Immigrants: The Challenge for Unions in Contemporary California.* Ithaca: Cornell University Press.

———. 2006. *LA Story: Immigrant Workers and the Future of the US Labor Movement.* New York: Russell Sage Foundation.

Milkman, Ruth, and Stephanie Luce. 2016. *State of the Unions 2016: A Profile of Organized Labor in New York City, New York State, and the United States.* New York: Joseph S. Murphy Institute for Worker Education and Labor Studies.

Milkman, Ruth, and Kim Voss. 2004. *Rebuilding Labor: Organizing and Organizers in the New Union Movement.* Ithaca: Cornell University Press.

Moberg, David. 2015. "The Union Behind the Biggest Campaign Against Walmart in History May Be Throwing in the Towel, Why?" *In These Times,* August 11. Accessed July 23, 2016. http://inthesetimes.com/article/18271/which-way-our-walmart.

Moreton, Bethany. 2010. *To Serve God and Wal-Mart: The Making of a Christian Free Enterprise.* Boston: Harvard University Press.

Moody, Kim. 1997. *Workers in a Lean World: Unions in the International Economy*. London: Verso.

——. 2007. *US Labor in Trouble and Transition: The Failure of Reform From Above, the Promise of Revival From Below*. London: Verso.

Moulian, Tomás. 2002. *Chile Actual: Anatomía de un Mito*. Santiago: LOM ediciones.

National Labor Relations Board. 2016. "Employee Rights." Accessed May 26, 2016. https://www.nlrb.gov/rights-we-protect/employee-rights.

Negocios Globales. 2016. "Industria Logística: En la Búsqueda de Crecimiento en 2016." Accessed May 26, 2016. http://www.emb.cl/negociosglobales/articulo.mvc?xid=2467&tip=3&xit=industria-logistica-en-la-busqueda-del-crecimiento-en-2016.

No Al Plan Laboral blog. 2015. "Reforma Laboral: Un Gran Retroceso Para Todos Los Trabajadores Chilenos." Accessed September 9, 2016. https://noalplanlaboral.com/el-Proyecto-de-ley/.

Nuñez, Daniel. 2009. "El Movimiento de los trabajadores contratistas de CODELCO: Una experiencia innovadora de negociación colectiva." In *El renacer de la huelga obrera en Chile: El movimiento sindical en la primera decada del siglo Xxi*, pp. 37–74. Santiago: Instituto de Ciencias Alejandro Lipschultz.

Offe, Claus, and Helmut Wiesenthal. 1980. "Two Logics of Collective Action: Theoretical Notes on Social Glass and Organizational Form." *Political Power and Social Theory* 1(1): 67–115.

Olney, Peter. 2015. "Where Did OUR Walmart Campaign Go Wrong?" *In These Times*, December 14. Accessed January 15, 2016. http://inthesetimes.com/working/entry/18692/our-walmart-union-ufcw-black-friday.

Organization for Economic Cooperation and Development (OECD). 2013. "Government at Glance: Chile Country Fact Sheet." Accessed January 15, 2015. https://www.oecd.org/gov/GAAG2013_CFS_CHL.pdf.

——. 2015. "Trade Union Density." Accessed January 15, 2016. https://stats.oecd.org/Index.aspx?DataSetCode=UN_DEN.

Ossandón, Jose. 2014. "Sowing Consumers in the Garden of Mass Retailing in Chile." *Consumption, Markets, and Culture* 17(5): 429–47.

Ostalé, Enrique. 2011. Testimony at South African Competition Tribunal Hearings, Johannesburg.

OUR Walmart. 2014. "Respect the Bump." Accessed August 12, 2016. http://forrespect.org/.

Palacios-Valladares, Indira. 2011. *Industrial Relations after Pinochet: Firm Level Unionism and Collective Bargaining Outcomes in Chile*. New York: Peter Lang.

Palma, Alexis. 2008. *Explaining Earnings and Income Inequality in Chile*. Doctoral Thesis. Department of Economics, Göteborg University.

Parker, Mike, and Martha Gruelle. 1999. *Democracy Is Power: Building Unions from the Bottom Up*. Detroit: Labor Notes.

Pérez, Domingo. 2014. "Las Formas de la Huelga en el Chile Actual: Análisis Cuantitativo y Mapeo de la Acción y la Masa Huelguísticas." M.A. thesis, Santiago: Universidad de Chile.

Piven, Frances Fox, and Richard A. Cloward. 1978. *Poor People's Movements: Why They Succeed, How They Fail*. New York: Vintage Books.

Qureshi, Lubna Z. 2008. *Nixon, Kissinger, and Allende: U.S. Involvement in the 1973 Coup in Chile.* New York: Rowman & Littlefield.

Reid, Joseph D., and Michael M. Kurth. 1984. "The Contribution of Exclusive Representation to Union Strength." *Journal of Labor Research* 5(4): 391–412.

Riquelme Giagnoni, Veronica, and Abarca Ferrando. 2015. "Mas Mujeres en los Sindicatos: Sectores con Alta Sindicalizacion Feminina." Dirección de Trabajo Working Paper.

Rosado Marzán, César. 2010. "Of Labor Inspectors and Judges: Chilean Labor Law Enforcement after Pinochet (And What the U.S. Can Do to Help)," *St. Louis University Law Journal* (54): 497–524 (symposia essay).

Ruminot, Nelson. 2009. "La Huelga en Forestal Arauco: De Las Acciones Sindicales al Forzamiento de la Negociación Colectiva Inter-Empresa." In *El Renacer de la Huelga Obrera en Chile: El Movimiento Sindical en la Primera Decada del Siglo XXI*, pp.117–34. Santiago: Instituto de Ciencias Alejandro Lipschultz.

Schneider, Cathy. 1995. *Shantytown Protest in Pinochet's Chile.* Philadelphia: Temple University Press.

Schnitzer, Yael. 2011. "Malas Practicas Laborares de Wal-Mart Atterizan en Chile." *El Mostrador*, March 25. Accessed April 11, 2011. http://www.elmostrador.cl/noticias/pais/2011/03/25/malas-practicas-laborales-de-wal-mart-aterrizan-en-chile/.

Seidman, Gay W. 2007. *Beyond the Boycott: Labor Rights, Human Rights, and Transnational Activism: Labor Rights, Human Rights, and Transnational Activism.* New York: Russell Sage Foundation.

——. 2008. "Transnational Labour Campaigns: Can the Logic of the Market be Turned against Itself?" *Development and Change* 39(6): 991–1003.

Selvin, David F. 1996. *A Terrible Anger: The 1934 Waterfront and General Strikes in San Francisco.* Detroit: Wayne State University Press.

Sindicato de Trabajadores Bodegas LTS. 2010. *Contando Nuestra Historia "Llena de Lucha y Dignidad."* Santiago: Transnational Information Exchange.

Sindicato Empresa Líder Express-Plaza Italia blog. 2008. "Análisis del Acuerdo Marco Suscrito por DyS con el Sindicato Interempresa." Accessed September 14, 2015. https://sindicatolider65.blogspot.com.

Sindicato Interempresa Líder. 2008. "Acuerdo Marco."

Sharpe, Teresa. 2004. "Union Democracy and Successful Campaigns: The Dynamics of Staff Authority and Worker Participation in an Organizing Union." In *Rebuilding Labor: Organizing and Organizers in the New Union Movement*, edited by Ruth Milkman and Kim Voss, pp.62–87. Ithaca: Cornell University Press.

Shorrock, Tim. 2003. "Labor's Cold War." *The Nation*, May 1. Accessed July 14, 2016. https://www.thenation.com/article/labors-cold-war/.

Silver, Beverly J. 2003. *Forces of Labor: Workers' Movements and Globalization since 1870.* Cambridge: Cambridge University Press.

Stallings, Barbara. 1978. *Class Conflict and Economic Development in Chile, 1958–1973.* Palo Alto: Stanford University Press.

Stecher, Antonio. 2012. "Perfiles Identitarios de Trabajadores de Grandes Empresas del Retail en Santiago de Chile: Aportes Psicosociales a la Comprensión de las Identidades Laborales." *Psykhe* 21: 29–20.

Stecher, Antonio, Lorena Godoy, and Juan Pablo Toro. 2010. "Condiciones y Experiencias de Trabajo en la Sala de Venta de un Supermercado: Explorando los Procesos de Flexibilización Laboral en el Sector del Retail en Chile." *Polis* 27: 1–23.

Stepan-Norris, Judith. 1997. "The Making of Union Democracy." *Social Forces* 72(2): 475–510.

Stepan-Norris, Judith, and Maurice Zeitlin. 1989. " 'Who Gets the Bird?' or, How the Communists Won Power and Trust in America's Unions: The Relative Autonomy of Intraclass Political Struggles." *American Sociological Review* 54(4): 503–23.

———. 1996. "Insurgency, Radicalism, and Democracy in America's Industrial Unions." *Social Forces* 75(1): 1–32.

Stillerman, Joel. 1998. "The Paradoxes of Power: The Unintended Consequences of Military Rule for Chilean Working-Class Mobilization." *Political Power and Social Theory* 12: 97–140.

———. 2004. "Disciplined Workers and Avid Consumers: Neoliberal Policy and the Transformation of Work and Identity among Chilean Metal Workers." In *Victims of the Chilean Miracle: Workers and Neoliberalism in the Pinochet Era, 1973–2002*, edited by Peter Winn, pp. 164–208. Durham: Duke University Press.

———. 2010. "The Contested Spaces of Chile's Middle Classes." *Political Power and Social Theory* 21: 209–38.

———. 2012. "Chile's Forgotten Consumers: Poor Urban Families, Consumption Strategies, and the Moral Economy of Risk in Santiago." In *Consumer Culture in Latin America*, edited by Anna Cristina Petierra and John Sinclair, pp. 67–80. New York: Palgrave Macmillan.

Stillerman, Joel, and Rodrigo Salcedo. 2012. "Transposing the Urban to the Mall: Routes, Relationships, and Resistance in Two Santiago, Chile, Shopping Centers." *Journal of Contemporary Ethnography* 41(3): 309–36.

Tilly, Chris. 2006. "Wal-Mart and Its Workers: NOT the Same All Over the World." *Connecticut Law Review* 39(4): 1805–23.

Tinsman, Heidi. 2014. *Buying into the Regime: Grapes and Consumption in Cold War Chile and the United States*. Durham: Duke University Press.

Torche, Florencia. 2005. "Unequal but Fluid: Social Mobility in Chile in Comparative Perspective." *American Sociological Review* 70(3): 422–50.

Turrini, Joseph. 1997. "The Newton Steel Strike: A Watershed in the CIO's Failure to Organize 'Little Steel.' " *Labor History* 38(2–3): 229–65.

Tyler, Phillip, and Melissa Hancock. 2001. *Work, Postmodernism, and Organization: A Critical Introduction*. London: Sage.

Ugarte, Jose Luis, and Sergio Gamonal. 2015. "La Gran Reformita Laboral." *El Mostrador*, January 11. Accessed June 22, 2016. http://www.elmostrador.cl/noticias/opinion/2015/01/11/la-gran-reformita-laboral/.

Urrutia, Miguel. 2015. *Nuevas Formas y Horizontes de Politización Sindical en el Marco De Conflictors Laborales: Un Estudio Exploratorio en la Región Metropolitana de Valparaíso y del Bío-Bío*. Santiago: Centro de Investigación Político Social del Trabajo.

Valdivia Court. 2010. T-11-2010 [Juzgado de Trabajo de Valdivia].

Valenzuela, Julio. 1976. "The Chilean Labor Movement: The Institutionalization of Conflict." In *Chile: Politics and Society*, edited by Arturo Valenzuela and J. Samuel Valenzuela, pp. 135–71. New Brunswick, NJ: Rutgers University Press.

Van Bavel, Rene, and Lucia Sell Trujillo. 2003. "Understandings of Consumerism in Chile." *Journal of Consumer Culture* 3(3): 343–62.

Verdugo, Patricia. 2003. *Allende: Cómo la Casa Blanca Provocó su Muerte*. Barcelona: Catalonia.

Vergara, Juan. 2016. "Reforma laboral (XXIII): Recuento de los Retrocesos de la 'Reforma Histórica.'" *Prosindical*. http://www.prosindical.cl/reforma-laboral-xxiii-recuento-de-los-retrocesos-de-la-reforma-historica/.

Villagra, Rodrigo. 2010. "Prólogo." In *Contando Nuestra Historia "Llena de Lucha y Dignidad,"* pp. 1–2. Santiago: Transnational Information Exchange.

Voss, Kim. 2010. "Democratic Dilemmas: Union Democracy and Union Renewal." *Transfer: European Review of Labour and Research* 16(3): 369–82.

Voss, Kim, and Pablo Gaston. 2014. "Neoliberal Dilemmas." Paper presented at the American Sociological Association Conference, San Francisco, August.

Voss, Kim, and Rachel Sherman. 2000. "Breaking the Iron Law of Oligarchy: Union Revitalization in the American Labor Movement." *American Journal of Sociology* 106(2): 303–49.

Walchuk, Brad. 2011. "Union Democracy and Labour Rights: A Cautionary Tale." *Global Labour Journal* 2(2). Accessed June 12, 2013. https://escarpmentpress.org/globallabour/article/view/1099.

Walmart. 2011. "Codigo de Etica." Accessed June 12, 2013. www.dys.cl.

——. 2013. "Bodegas." Accessed April 12, 2014. www.dys.cl.

——. 2014. "Worldwide Stores." Accessed May 21, 2015. https://corporate.walmart.com/our-story/our-locations.

——. 2015. "Worldwide Stores." Accessed September 1, 2016. https://corporate.walmart.com/our-story/our-locations.

Weinbaum, Eve S. 2004. *To Move a Mountain: Fighting the Global Economy in Appalachia*. New York: New Press.

Winn, Peter. 1986. *Weavers of Revolution: The Yarur Workers and Chile's Road to Socialism*. New York: Oxford University Press.

——. 2004. "No Miracle for Us: The Textile Industry in the Pinochet Era, 1973–1998." In *Victims of the Chilean Miracle: Workers and Neoliberalism in the Pinochet Era, 1973–2002*, edited by Peter Winn, pp. 125–63. Durham: Duke University Press.

Wolkowitz, Carol. 2006. *Bodies at Work*. London: Sage.

World Bank. 2016. "Labor Force Participation Rate, Female." Accessed November 16, 2016. http://data.worldbank.org/indicator/SL.TLF.CACT.FE.ZS?locations=CL.

Wright, Erik Olin. 2000. "Working-Class Power, Capitalist-Class Interests, and Class Compromise." *American Journal of Sociology* 105(4): 957–1002.

Yates, Charlotte. 2006. "Challenging Misconceptions about Organizing Women into Unions." *Gender, Work & Organization* 13(6): 565–84.

INDEX

Lightning Source UK Ltd.
Milton Keynes UK
UKOW01n0602080218
317556UK00008B/471/P